Go! M

How to Implement Ministries That Get Results

By H. Justin Reyes and Dr. Daniel Boyd

Dear Linda & Bill,

Peace be with you. I hope you are well. I hope you find in these pages even more inspiration to keep making disciples.

In Christ,
Daniel

ISBN 979-8-5623-7798-2 (paperback)

Illustrations by Genevieve Fable

First Printing, 2020

DEDICATIONS

Justin

In dedication to Mother Church and Mama Mary. Thank you to the many priests who have guided me and friends/mentors from other faith traditions. Thank you to my parents, who introduced me to the faith, my beautiful wife who always supports me, and my children. Thank you, Dan for saying "yes" to this great adventure and being a friend and confidante. Above all, "Blessed be the God and Father of our Lord Jesus Christ, who in his great mercy gave us a new birth to a living hope through the resurrection of Jesus Christ from the dead," 1 Peter 1:3

Dan

"But when the kindness and generous love of God our Savior appeared... he saved us" (Titus 3:4-5). To our good and loving God be all the glory, all the praise, all the honor.

It has been a blessing to write this book, for Him, with my good friend Justin. Thank you for the invitation to co-create with you. To my friends and family who offered feedback and prayers, thank you, and please be assured of my prayers for you. And to my beautiful wife and daughter who patiently supported me along the way, my heart is yours. Thank you.

Acknowledgements

To Regina, Laura, Brandon, Lynne, Christy, Kelly, Amanda, Rachel, Jason, Father Jacob, Carl (Dad), and Jason, thank you for the gift of your time. Your feedback helped us to craft this book. We are grateful to you for your friendship, encouragement, and prayers. Please be assured of ours.

TABLE OF CONTENTS

PASTORAL GROWTH

END NOTES

Abbreviations

CCC - Catechism of the Catholic Church, 2020 Edition

EG - Evangelii Gaudium (Pope Francis)

EN - Evangelii Nuntiandi (Pope Paul VI)

RM - Redemptoris Missio (Pope John Paul II)

US - Ubicumque et sempter (Pope Benedict XVI)

FOREWORD
By Brandon Vogt

One of the most exciting developments in the Church over the last few decades has been the growing number of Catholics waking up to the urgency of evangelization and discipleship. Throughout the first half of the twentieth century, most Church institutions were full and thriving. Schools were packed, priests were abundant, laypeople were crammed in pews, and religious orders enjoyed waves of vocations. But in the second half of the century, walloped by the turbulent sexual and cultural revolutions and the massive tsunami of secularism, many Catholics walked away. Priests and religious left their communities, schools emptied out, and parishes saw a massive exodus of men, women, and children. A couple decades into the twentieth century, we're still reeling from all that damage and loss.

However, this book isn't about analyzing the devastating problem of attrition, why so many people have given up on the Church. It's about the solution: effective evangelization and discipleship. As the authors say in the beginning, "This book is our attempt to help refocus our efforts on what matters and what works. The high impact approach we need is to make disciples."

Most parishes and ministries are aware of these challenges--disaffiliation, disengagement, dwindling knowledge about and passion for the faith--and with good wills and hearts, they attempt various solutions. Some suggest we need more programs. Or more creative marketing! Or more food and entertainment! But while those attempts are usually well-meaning, they often fail because they aren't matched with thoughtful planning, strategy, and analysis. Their hearts are in the right place, and there's plenty of excitement, but they're often missing an adequate framework for success.

That's where this book shines. Its goal is to refocus our evangelical efforts on solutions that work, by providing practical, flexible, and proven approaches to ministry. Using examples from their own years in ministry, along with adapting strategies from the outside worlds of business, marketing, and strategic planning, they've provided a roadmap for planning successful ministry, assessing its effectiveness, adapting on the fly, and reaching our goals, both our immediate ministry goals and the ultimate aim of introducing people to Jesus Christ through his Church.

One of the important paradigm shifts they recommend is beginning with the "Flock Experience," which means "starting with the lost sheep in mind, putting ourselves into their shoes." This involves building our ministry or parish specifically for non-Catholics and fallen-away Catholics, considering what they need in order to come back to the Lord, rather than what we want in a ministry experience. This framework encourages us to ask questions such as, what will they think when they visit our parish website? Will they feel welcomed or ignored? How about when they visit our parish or ministry for the first time? Will they be noticed and engaged, or ignored and dismissed? What about the content of our ministry? Is it primarily designed to satisfy already-committed Catholics, or does it have an evangelical aim, meant to attract and develop new followers of Christ? This concept of "Flock Experience" can revolutionize the orientation of most parishes and ministries.

You'll also find how this book helpfully walks you through, hand in hand, the entire process of discipleship, providing sample questions, checklists, and timelines to help launch and run a successful ministry. The result is turn-key evangelization. They've provided the framework--you just need to execute it. I'm especially glad to see such a strong emphasis on the pre- and post-launch stages of ministry, which are often ignored. Many times, when Catholics start new evangelical initiatives, we spend all of our time doing ministry. But we should devote adequate time to thinking about, preparing, and planning these efforts, and then evaluating their effectiveness at the end. Christ calls us to be "wise as serpents and innocent as doves" (Mt 10:16), and many of us get the second part right. We bring an innocent and hopeful spirit to new ministry ideas. But unless we also bring wisdom, that innocence devolves into ineffective naivete. We need to think, plan, and strategize. This book shows how to do that.

I'm hopeful that after reading this book, you'll finish not just inspired and excited about your ministry, but confident in what to do moving forward. You'll know the right questions to ask, the right steps to take, and the right tools to measure success. You'll know how to make disciples.

CHAPTER 1

BACK ON TRACK

High Impact

In 2009, New Zealand native and educational researcher John Hattie released a monumental publication titled *Visible Learning*.[i] In his book, Hattie outlined a novel argument for the education community: everything you are doing works. Wait . . . what? Everything? Yes—or at least, nearly everything. Educators have long pointed to any type of academic growth as proof of success even when it was clear that some students suffered under their teachers' tutelage.

So, did Hattie confirm what everyone already knew? Actually, he did the opposite. Hattie was wise enough to recognize that children will almost always learn something in a school setting. A five-year-old who starts kindergarten in the fall and leaves ten months later will know more and score higher on standardized exams. Imagine that! A child is noticeably smarter after a period of maturation that is a sizable fraction of their entire life!

The problem is not that what the teachers are doing doesn't work, but that some things only work *a little*. Hattie compared hundreds of different teaching strategies and ranked them by how much the strategy increased learning over an academic year. This created a rank order of strategies with some scoring high, others low, and a lot around the average mark.

What he found out was astounding. The many tried-and-true teaching methods (like homework) that so many teachers swore by were actually *below average*, meaning that they "worked," but other teaching methods had a larger impact on student learning. Students who were taught with less-than-average strategies still learned; *they just learned less* than they could have.

Busy, but Efficient?

Unfortunately, we don't have a John Hattie who has ranked the various types of ministries in the Church. Nonetheless, the paradigm shift that Hattie ushered in is helpful for us, too.

Are we producing results? Yes, but when we look around do we always see the most effective ministry models? Have we become so accustomed to sub-optimal results in ministry that we are happy to accept any spiritual growth as evidence that we are doing the right thing?

Anyone who has seen recent research reports about dis-affiliation rates in the Catholic Church knows that we are not always getting it right. "Catholicism has experienced a greater net loss due to religious switching than has any other religious tradition in the U.S."[ii] According to recent PEW survey data, for every one person who enters the Catholic Church through the RCIA, over six leave the Church. We need high-impact and high-yield more than ever before. We wrote this book to try to help achieve that.

We need a Hattie-like paradigm shift in the way we look at our ministries and the way we live as Catholics. Yes, LOTS of different ministries are beneficial. The tried-and-true or age-old groups, clubs, and organizations still do lots of good. But are they doing *as much* good as we need them to do? Are they high-impact and high-yield at a time when our ministries need to produce at a high level? Or are they just average, or worse, below average?

While it is a stark thing to say, we would argue that for all of our effort we are failing at our main mission. In the last ten years, we have lost 10% of the general Catholic population and 33% of the millennial Catholic population (Pew Research, 2019).[iii]

There is a peculiar paradox in congressional approval ratings that might explain why more Catholics are not concerned. Most Americans have a higher approval rating of their own congressional representative than they do of Congress as a whole.[iv] In other words, we think Congress is doing poorly, but our own representative is doing just fine. If we had to guess, this is probably because we don't like to admit that the power to fix the problem is in our own hands.

Perhaps something like this is going on in our own parishes and dioceses. There is clear evidence that the Church is in trouble, but do we feel enough urgency to accept major change in our own Catholic backyard? Again, it seems like we as Catholics are ready for some kind of change, but do we know where we want to go and how to get there?

This book is our attempt to help refocus our efforts on what matters and what works. The high-impact approach we need is to make disciples. This is the big picture. By refocusing our efforts on this and providing practical, flexible, and proven approaches to ministry, we believe that we will grow by attracting new Catholics and making sure others never leave.

Make Disciples

So how will this book help you make disciples? In these pages, we offer focused and easy-to-learn concepts, many of which are adapted from the worlds of education and business and illustrated with stories from the field of ministry. We will help you stay focused on what really matters, ask the right questions, and move towards tangible ministry success. You will create plans with realistic dates and identify the proper channels to reach your audience. You will also learn how to create checklists that make event execution a cinch. We will also help you create the type of team you want in your ministry. We are confident that this book will help you in the Great Commission of making the Gospel known to the whole world.

Our True North: Evangelization

In pathfinding, navigating, and geography, true north differs slightly from magnetic north by a small margin. For most people, the variance is so slim that it makes no difference. But, if success depends on knowing *precisely* where you need to go, knowing true north is essential. For us, our true north is the only way forward. We can no longer settle for anything but high-impact ministry efforts because anything less means not fulfilling the mission the Lord has set before us. Getting things almost right will not be sufficient because we are motivated by the love of God. Love is never satisfied with *almost*, but with consummate completion.

So, what is our true north as Catholics? We believe we find the answer in Jesus's last words to His disciples. In Matthew 28:19-20, just right prior to the Ascension, Jesus tells His disciples, "Go therefore and make disciples of all nations . . . teaching them to observe all that I have commanded you." We are pretty good at teaching everything Jesus has commanded, but we spend much of our time teaching people who already know, rather than people who have never heard about Jesus. What about making disciples of all nations? This is like if a teacher only wanted to work with the gifted and honor students who already love learning while ignoring the children who need the most help!

If we are looking for the home-run-hitting, perfect-tens-all-round approach, we believe the answer is to be found in the last commandment of Jesus: be intentional about inviting and forming people to follow Him. Some pretty smart people agree with us. Except for the short-lived John Paul I, all of the Popes since the Second Vatican Council have been univocal in calling for a renewal of the Catholic Church's fundamental missionary orientation, a renewal of the Great Commission of Jesus Christ.

Following the close of Vatican II in 1965, Paul VI said that the sum of the mission of Jesus was to announce the Gospel and that all of the "aspects of His mystery . . . were components of His evangelizing activity" (EN 6). The Holy Father was so bold as to say that even the "cross and the resurrection, the permanence of His presence [in the Eucharist]" were components in Christ's evangelical mission (EN 6). The whole of Christ's life was indistinguishable from His evangelical mission, so much so that Paul VI could say, "Evangelizing is . . . the vocation proper to the Church, her deepest identity. She exists to evangelize . . . (EN 14), and "thus it is the whole Church that receives the mission to evangelize, and the work of *each individual member* is important for the whole" (EN 15, *emphasis added*).

Echoing the words of Paul VI in his 1990 encyclical *Re-*

demptoris Missio, St. John Paul II reiterated that "[t]he missionary thrust therefore belongs to the very nature of the Christian life" (RM 1). If it is true that "[the Church] cannot do other than proclaim the Gospel" (RM 5, 3) we dare to say that if we don't evangelize, we have failed to grasp what it means to be Christian.

Pope Benedict XVI, reinforcing the importance of the New Evangelization initiated by his predecessor saint, established a Pontifical Council for Promoting the New Evangelization with his 2010 Apostolic Letter and Motu Proprio, *Ubicumque et semper*. In the opening paragraph, the Holy Father reminded the Church that "the mission of evangelization . . . is necessary for the Church: it cannot be overlooked; it is an expression of her very nature."

In our present time, Pope Francis has been crystal clear in calling for all Catholics to engage in evangelization, reminding us of the words of His predecessor St. John Paul II, "there must be no lessening of the impetus to preach the Gospel . . . this is the first task of the Church" (EG 15, citing RM 34). Pope Francis issued us this challenge, "What would happen if we were to take these words seriously? We would realize that missionary outreach is *[the model] for all the Church's activity*" (EG 15).

If evangelization is an expression of the very nature of the Church, then when we don't evangelize, we are presenting a false image of the Church. The Church that Christ started is one that goes out to proclaim the Good News. If we fail or refuse to do that, then what are we saying? That the news isn't good? That we don't think it is worth sharing?

In one sense, the Church ceases to make sense precisely when we cease evangelizing. If this message isn't worth spreading, why would anyone stay? One of the many reasons that evangelizing is high impact is because it is an authentic expression of the Church, a witness to the truth of the Gospel. Everyone, especially young people and non-Catholics, will absolutely question the value of the Catholic faith if we don't attempt to live that same faith to the fullest. If parents, catechists, parish leaders, deacons, and priests were intentional about sharing the faith, then young people would see a real-life commitment to the Gospel of Jesus. This alone might not stop them from leaving, but it would at least say to them that we take the faith seriously, even the parts that are challenging and risky.

The Other Side of the Boat: Missionary Discipleship

So, we've established that the Church's primary mission is to evangelize. But evangelize for what? To make better-behaving Christians? To make people who know the faith well? To help people be happy?

In the Church, perhaps our biggest challenge is our perceived scope of mission. There is a university-sized library worth of documents written on liturgy, social justice, catechesis, mission work, and theology. One could be forgiven for thinking that the primary job of a Catholic is first to learn and then to do . . . everything that they read about. There are always shelters, food pantries, and missions that need volunteers and donations. Every parish needs more catechists and every choir, more singers. There are sick people to visit and to whom we must bring the Eucharist, bingo games to assist with, auctions and rummage sales to staff, and the list goes on.

Now don't get us wrong; we're not saying that the above activities are non-essential. Of course not! But if everything is a priority, nothing is a priority. And if we have a lengthy litany of volunteer opportunities, we are probably more likely to choose the ones that make us feel good, fit our schedule, or are easiest to accomplish. How many people would willingly choose to talk to a non-Catholic about their faith instead of to help run the beer tent at the fall festival? Not that you couldn't do both, but most of us would choose the beer tent.

If we want to see our numbers turn around, we have to make hard choices and sacrifice our favorite ministries for the central ones. Based on Jesus's teaching and the witness of the Apostles, this means helping other people to see and fall in love with Jesus and accept His Good News, especially as it is lived and experienced in the Catholic Church.

At the close of John's Gospel and after the resurrection, Jesus appears to the disciples while they are fishing. From the beach, He calls out, "Children, have you caught anything to eat?" (John 21:5). Of course, He already knows the answer: they haven't caught anything. He instructs them to cast the net on the right side of the boat. The resulting catch was so great that the disciples couldn't haul it in themselves! The fishermen that He had appointed fishers of men had been laboring without success. We hear in this passage an echo of how we find ourselves today.

If we have a "right side" of the boat today, we believe it is a recommitment to missionary discipleship. Missionary discipleship has been the subject of recent books, blog posts, podcasts, and conference proposals, yet it has not fully taken root. One consulting agency we spoke to in 2019 told us that their research indicated as few as 25,000 U.S. Catholics engage in true evangelization. To paraphrase G.K. Chesterton, missionary discipleship "has not been tried and found wanting. It has been found difficult; and left untried."[v] So what makes missionary discipleship the "right side" of the boat? Because it is the clear command from Jesus, and when we abide in Him, He promises that we will bear fruit (John 15:5). It is also the clarion guidance from the Church: we exist to make disciples (EN 14). If making disciples isn't high impact, nothing is.

Is Results-Based Ministry Contrary to Authentic Christianity?

If we were only interested in converting people for the sake of keeping score, filling the pews and coffers, or stroking our own ego, then yes, it would be wrong to focus on the numbers. But that problem would not be in the numbers—it would be in our hearts. The Gospel must always be about Jesus because it is His Good News, not ours. He asked us to tell everyone and He gave us assurances that He would help us to be successful. "[If] you have faith the size of a mustard seed, you will say to this mountain, 'Move from here to there,' and it will move. Nothing will be impossible for you" (Matt 17:20-21). "Everything is possible to one who has faith" (Mark 9:23). "Take courage, I have conquered the world" (John 16:33).

Can we find results-based ministry in scripture? We think so. "If the house is worthy, let your peace come upon it; if not, let your peace return to you. Whoever will not receive you or listen to your words—go outside that house or town and shake the dust from your feet" (Matt 10:13-14). This verse is directly related to missionary discipleship as it is part of the instructions Jesus gives to the twelve when He sends them out on mission to proclaim the Good News (Matt 10:7). If someone's heart is open, stay a while and continue to form disciples. If not, we move on and find someone else who is ready to listen. Those are His words, not ours. What is one possible interpretation? Get busy and spread the word (Or *Go! Make Disciples!*)!

Similarly, when Jesus comes to His home town and begins to preach, the people do not accept Him, and so He does just a few miracles and moves on to others who are open (Mark 6:5-6). What are the criteria for deciding whether to stay and continue sharing the Good News with someone? Openness to Christ. Not a sophisticated metric, but an easy one to work with. And the tacit belief here is that Christians will actually be going out and talking to people. It is clear from Jesus's own example that there is an urgency to be on the move and make things happen. He isn't exactly giving us evangelization quotas to fulfill, and we want to be clear that we aren't saying to focus on numbers. What we are saying is that if we get back to making disciples, the numbers will come.

What If?

Earlier, we referenced a passage from *Evangelii Gaudium* in which Pope Francis posed the question, "What would happen if the Church took its missionary vocation seriously?" (EG 15). The Church would grow—that is what would happen! While we recognize that it takes bravado to present this goal, would it be too much to ask that we as a Church strive for just one-percent growth per year? What if in a diocese of one million Catholics, we could gain ten thousand new Catholics every year? Across the country, this would be an increase of around six hundred thousand? This would mean so much more for the Church than just new members every year. This would mean more committed families, leading to more committed disciples evangelizing the world, as committed Catholic parents are the strongest force to help young Catholics keep the faith.

We don't think it is unreasonable to believe that we are

only ten years away from a complete turnaround for the Catholic Church in the United States (or anywhere). In ten years, we could have a generation of trained missionary disciples and asking for something as little as one-percent growth in the Church would be easy. We could expect our new Catholics to continue bringing others into the Church, and that these new converts would hand the faith on to their own children. It's hard to imagine sacramental marriages, baptisms, and participation in sacramental preparation going down, as has been the case for at least the past ten years if we achieved one-percent growth.

So how do we get there? Again, by re-focusing on the Great Commission as our true north and recognizing that making disciples *is* the high-impact approach we need. The remainder of this book will show you how to put this into practice, providing proven, flexible, and practical approaches. Together, let's go and make disciples for the Lord!

CHAPTER 2

GRAB THE KEYS

"I can't find my keys," is a common phrase in most households. For you jokesters out there, "Have you tried looking for them?" is not the best response, especially to an angry spouse. Trust us. But seriously, we have probably all lost our keys and there was that one person in our house growing up who ALWAYS lost keys.

Sometimes we lose the keys to ministry. We get caught up in the cyclical, non-stop life of a parish, a school, or other ministry and put off until another day what is truly essential. What should we do about this? Is there a purpose-driven key hook we can hang just inside the door to our office? No, but we have something better: anchor frameworks.

What is a framework anyway? We define it as a way to view ministry. These lenses work by highlighting the things that are hidden in plain sight, the things we may have been accidentally ignoring.

In this chapter, we present three anchor frameworks: Flock Experience, Discipleship Funnel, and Iterative Model. These will help block out interruptions and keep us focused on what's most important, namely, fulfilling the Great Commission. In the following chapters, we will introduce implementation frameworks you can apply directly to current and future ministries. Those frameworks are about *doing* ministry, whereas these first three contain overarching principles for how to *think* about ministry. They are not "pen-to-paper" like the implementation ones but are nonetheless essential. Before you start doing ministry, you need to make sure you are thinking about it the right way.

Flock Experience

In 1 Cor 9:19-23, Saint Paul wrote that he became all things to all people in order that he might win some for Christ. Similarly, in Acts 10, Saint Peter had a dream in which he saw a sheet come down with all manner of unclean animals upon it. He then heard the voice of the Lord saying, "Slaughter and eat (Acts 10:13). The Lord later explained to Saint Peter that the dream meant there were no unclean people (or food, thanks be to God for that dream!), and that the Apostles must be prepared to go to everyone.

Where both of these scripture passages point us is an approach to ministry where we focus on and adapt ourselves to the people who most need to hear the Gospel. Who are these people? According to Jesus, they are the sick, the sinners, and the lost sheep. Like many of us, Peter was initially focused only on those within the Church. It wasn't until he received the vision in Acts 10 that he understood his call to make the Gospel known to everyone. Jesus is calling us to do the same.

The Flock Experience is all about starting with the lost sheep in mind, putting ourselves into their shoes. It means that we build our ministry for them and what they need in order to come to the Lord, rather than what we want in a ministry experience. We like the expression, "Lock onto Lost Sheep!" This means that our sole focus is bringing the Gospel to those people who need it the most, period.

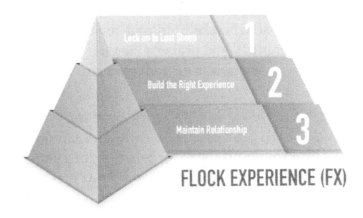

FLOCK EXPERIENCE (FX)

To use an example from Pope Francis, the Church is a field hospital, and in a field hospital you aren't worried about cholesterol and blood pressure. You are worried about the person who just walked in with shrapnel in his leg or some other life-threatening injury. You apply life-saving aid to those who need it before attending to the lesser needs of others. What does this mean? Our focus should be on those who are most in danger of dying without accepting the Gospel! This is the first and foundational step in the Flock Experience framework pyramid above. You identify those who are most in need of the Gospel and you create your ministry plan with them in mind. Remember, ministry is not about us and what we want. Ministry is about the people we want to serve. We should keep them at the forefront of our mind, building experiences to reach them, and not to make us feel good about ourselves.

The next step is to plan every aspect of your ministry so as to maximize chances for success. Now, scripture is very clear that it is the Lord who does the work, not us (1 Cor 3:7). We are but "unprofitable servants" after all (Luke

17:10). But we also find in the words of Jesus a reason to aim for success! Consider the example of the parable of the talents. Those who are bold and successful are given greater responsibility and praise, whereas "playing it safe" is met with a severe scolding and even the suggestion of hell.

So, what are we to do? We work prudently to ensure that our outreach gets results. Go through each step of the process, thinking about the experience of your flock. What will it be like for a real person? For example, if you were planning a conference, think about your intended audience or one of your "sheep." When they find out about the conference, what does the branding and marketing look like? How do they sign up? When they arrive, how are they greeted? What will they experience? Afterward, what is follow-up like? How will you keep in touch with them? Thinking about every step on the journey will help your sheep have the best experience possible. Just one misstep could be a deal-breaker (i.e.: they aren't greeted when they arrive, don't feel welcome, and decide to leave early).

So, we work prudently and efficiently to achieve our goal. We build our entire ministry with the single-minded purpose of ministering to and winning for Christ the lost sheep. This means we get very specific about whom we plan to minister to, then we build our experiences with those people in mind.

In addition to *whom*, we must know where and when we can find them, as well as when they will show up. Will young, disaffiliated Catholics show up to bingo on Friday night? Unclear. Will they participate in a social justice-related outreach? Maybe. Can you find them prowling niche groups on the internet in search of life's true meaning?

That's much more likely. Wherever they are, we should be, too? Remember, the Good Shepherd doesn't stay with the flock. He goes out to find those most in need of Him.

What does this look like in practice? Here is an example from one of the schools we worked in. The typical campus ministry model looks something like this: do one charitable drive a semester, one annual retreat per grade level, celebrate the liturgy once a month or once a week, offer reconciliation during Advent and Lent, and do what you can in between. This is a good foundation, but it offers a very undifferentiated experience to everyone.

I (Dan) used the Flock Experience framework to create an entirely different approach to ministry at a school where I once worked. Rather than offer one class retreat, this school offered nearly thirty small retreats—one for every varsity-sport's team and two retreats a year each for young men and young women. In the case of the team retreats, the first step in planning was to meet over lunch with team leaders and ask what they wanted. What did their team need, what did the captains want, what spiritual components or themes did they want to include? One team said reconciliation was important, as they had recently been experiencing unhealthy competition. Another said they wanted to work on trusting in the Lord as a source of mental peace. To begin to train the students to share their faith, the campus ministry staff then worked with the students to develop their own witness talks.

The entire retreat experience was planned around the needs, interests, and existing community/culture of a team. The campus ministry staff didn't try to pull students out of their comfort zone; rather, the staff went into the students' comfort zone to show the students how the Gospel enriches every aspect of their lives. Oh yeah, and the students also got to plan follow-up activities after the retreat so that the campus ministry staff could continue to engage the students in a meaningful way. After four years of these retreats, the students had quite the rapport with their campus ministry team!

Understanding your audience is key, and part of evangelization is knowing where people are naturally open to the Gospel as well as where they are more resistant. The goal is not to get them to agree to every single individual claim the Church has ever made. Rather, we share the core of the Gospel: God made us for a perfect relationship with Him; we ruined that relationship by sinning but Jesus came to earth, took on human flesh, suffered, died, and rose from the dead to restore us to a right relationship with the Father. If they can accept this, the grace of God will continue to act in their hearts to bring them to an increasing state of perfection.

Turning again to Saint Paul as the model for evangelists, did he follow the Flock Experience framework? Absolutely, and in at least two distinct scenarios. The first was in his work with gentiles. When many of the Jewish Christians insisted that pagan converts to Christianity had to adhere to Jewish law, Saint Paul saw the problem. How many grown men would accept Christianity if it meant circumcision? How about giving up bacon? Cheeseburgers?

Instead of insisting that his potential disciples adhere to Jewish law, when Paul encountered a different culture, he looked for the best way to proclaim the Good News. So, when he visited Athens and spoke in the Areopagus to the learned philosophers, he made an appeal to logos (Acts 17:16-34). Did it work for all of them? No, but it did work for some, including Dionysius, an early Christian convert whose faith we still know of today.

Discipleship Funnel

Comedian Steve Harvey once performed one of the best (in our opinion) introductions to Jesus ever, at least if Jesus were a professional athlete. If you want to check it out, just search "Steve Harvey titles of Jesus." It was so powerful, even *Steve* was moved by the Spirit. One of the titles that Harvey bestowed upon Jesus was record holder for the world's largest fish fry. Yes, Jesus gathered massive crowds, even upwards of 5000 when you include women and children (Matt 14:21). He also considered it worthwhile to spend much of His limited time alone with His three closest disciples. Why? Because this is how discipleship works. We didn't invent this concept, Jesus did. But we did name it, and we call it the Discipleship Funnel.

Discipleship Funnel

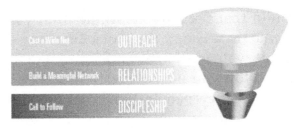

If the Flock Experience is about learning the best way to reach and connect with people, the Discipleship Funnel is about helping move those people from wherever they are in their relationship with God to the point of living as a mature disciple and witness of Jesus Christ. The Funnel starts wide, with outreach for large groups, perhaps hundreds or even thousands. The goal is to get on people's radar, begin to establish trust, and eventually build meaningful friendships. The Flock Experience gets you to this point, and the first stage in the Discipleship Funnel is to do something on a large scale that connects you with the target Flock. For example, one archdiocese in the US did this in 2019 with a large-scale discipleship event meant to attract everyone—Catholics and non-Catholics alike. Two years in advance, their Bishop asked every parish in the diocese not to schedule weddings or other major events on one weekend just so that all parish priests could attend with their flock. That was casting a wide net!

Next, the funnel gets a little narrower when you identify out of the whole crowd those who are ready to go a little deeper in their faith. You do this by building a meaningful network. Who are these people? They are the ones who show up and have the availability and the eagerness to do more, and you probably know whom we are talking about. The reason you cast the net is to identify these people who are ready to go deeper and form stronger relationships. "Many are invited, but few are chosen" (Matt 22:14).

How do you build that network? Working from your understanding of who these people are (Flock Experience), you offer small-scale, valuable experiences, community, formation, etc. that allow you and your team to make and deepen connections with new people. What this looks like depends on the Flock, but could include marriage workshops, parenting classes, Bible studies, or service opportunities.

Finally, the funnel narrows at the bottom. This is when you invite a small group of people, probably no more than eight and even as few as one, to an apprenticeship in following Jesus. If casting wide connects you with five hundred and building a meaningful network connects you with fifty, you will only call a handful to follow. How will you know who to choose? Just as in stage two, they will step forth of their own. More importantly, the Lord will make them known to you. Their open and seeking heart predisposes them to hear the word of God, and they will have both the time and the willingness to be led.

Practically, what does this look like? Scripture tells us in Acts 2:43-47. The followers of Jesus studied, worshipped, fellowshipped, and served together. They committed themselves to live as Jesus did and taught, they prayed together, they spent meaningful time as friends, and they provided for the needs of the community. In broad terms, this is how a disciple of Jesus lives. We will get into the practicality of this later, but as simple as it sounds, let's not lose sight of how radical, and attractive, this is. The reasons it is so powerful and transformative are many, but the simplest way to put it is that we begin to live like Christ. In living like Him and following in His footsteps, we start to learn through our very real human experience how sweet it is to be His disciple. We all know the difference between book learning and first-hand experience. Why should Christianity be any different?

Are we suggesting some form of elitism or exclusivity in the Church? No. But discipleship has to be person to person. You cannot mass produce followers of Jesus and this is why the funnel gets narrow at the end. People become disciples when you invest your time and energy into them.

Of course, if you already know the people you need to disciple you can skip steps one and two, but we can't overstate this point. One of the biggest reasons the Church is not growing right now is because we don't think it is a worthwhile investment to spend lots of time with a small number of people. Consider the parable of the sower and the seeds: when people first hear the word, they may initially get excited about their faith. But if we don't spend time apprenticing them as followers of Jesus, it is unlikely they will become mature disciples.

"But wait!" you say. "I want to make one hundred disciples!" You will. But start with ten and get them to make ten more apiece, and so forth. We do not want you to make a hundred disciples. We want you to help make millions or billions, and that means getting others to help along the way. And yes, we really do mean billions.

There Must Be a Faster Way!

Why can't we mass-produce disciples? There are lots of answers, but the best response is that not even Jesus could. He spent some time getting the word out to large crowds and He spent some of His time with medium-sized groups (Luke 10). But it seems like He spent the majority of His time with a small group of followers. Rather than try to tell everyone about the Good News Himself, His goal was to prepare others to share His message in word and in deed. To accomplish this, He apprenticed them in His Way. This was no cheap self-help seminar. He was inviting them to embark upon a radically different way of living. If Jesus did this, then it is good enough for us, too.

Authentic Friendship

Somewhere between building a meaningful network and calling others to follow, you will start to see the seeds of authentic friendship. This is fundamental and foundational in the discipleship process. It is what separates Catholic evangelization from proselytizing, and it is a critical step in becoming a mature disciple. This too is rooted in the model of Jesus, "I no longer call you slaves . . . I have called you friends" (John 15:15). Jesus developed meaningful relationships with His disciples and the clearest reason for this is that the Gospel is rooted in love. If we seek to love our neighbor, we cannot help but develop deep friendships with them, and the shared goal of spreading the Gospel will only strengthen that connection.

You will know when you are developing an authentic friendship when you ask someone to follow Christ—not to carve a notch in your belt or record a win, but because you desire for that other person to experience the love of God as you have. The Holy Spirit, your conscience, and your gut will tell you if you are being a friend or just using the person to feel good about yourself. Trust those three voices and don't be afraid to enter into authentic friendship!

If you can honestly desire for someone to share in the rich blessings of God, you can rest assured you are acting as a friend. On the other hand, if you are trying to make disciples for some other reason, then we suggest that you step back momentarily and spend some time in prayer with the Lord. Ask Him to reignite that fire within you and to remind you why you first felt compelled to share His story. What were those things that set your heart ablaze and can you find the desire to share that same goodness with others?

What Is the Point?

The goal of the Discipleship Funnel is to help connect disciple-makers with potential new disciples. When we call people into a small group or one-on-one apprenticeship as a disciple, we ultimately hope that they will go out and help us spread the Good News, making more disciples. Is this discipleship for the sake of discipleship? Don't we want more for this person than to simply become a sales rep for Jesus? Of course! The whole Discipleship Funnel is built on opportunities, outreach, and experiences that introduce people to the joy and freedom of living as a redeemed child of God.

The Iterative Model

An experiment was once done of pitting two groups against each other in a challenge to build a structure out of seemingly random items: business school students vs. kindergarteners. Each group was given a few materials to work with, with the goal of building the tallest free-standing structure possible in a given amount of time. The winners? The kindergartners. Why? The process they followed.

What did the business school students do when time began? They started talking, planning, and writing down how they would accomplish the task. They thought success would come from sufficient research and planning. But then when it came time to build, they kept having issues with their structures or ran out of time. What did the kindergarteners do? They spent a little bit of time discussing and then dove right in! Working together, having fun, and trying to build right away. Sure, they had lots of failures as they started, but they learned quickly through this iterative approach of trying, failing, learning, and trying again. Eventually, they found the right recipe for a sturdy structure and kept adding!

This story goes to show the importance of taking a little bit of time to plan, but then just diving in! Nowadays, we seem to want to research everything to avoid failure at all costs. But Our Lord gave us a different approach of being childlike and leaping right into action. Even St. Paul understands this process of maturation as he says in 1 Cor 13:11, "When I was a child, I used to . . . reason like a child." And while he goes on to say that as an adult he put off childish things, he arrived at that place of wisdom and understanding because of his willingness to learn and grow. Childhood is an age of mistakes, and it is, therefore, a time of growth and learning. Maybe this is just one more reason to be like a child before the Lord (Matt 18:3)!

One of the harshest sounding sayings of Jesus was when He said to enter a house and offer your peace. If they refuse it and your peace returns to you, you are to shake the dust from your feet and leave that house (Luke 10:5-6). A similar saying of Jesus was not to cast "your pearls before swine" (Matt 7:6). What we hear in both of these passages is to learn from your ministry experience and continue moving on, always growing and improving. Our third and final framework is the Iterative Model.

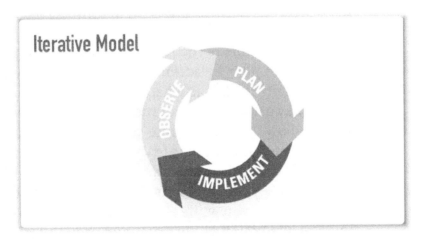

Quite simply, this means that you **plan**, **implement**, and **observe**. And you keep engaging in this cycle, doing your best to plan an engaging experience, giving it your all in the implementation phase, and then learning and improving for the future. You may have seen something like it in the past, and likely experienced it as a kid while playing with friends, but here's a quick walkthrough of each stage:

1. **Plan** – This is when you quickly decide what you are going to do. Now in the above example, we're not saying to be like the business school students and overdo this phase. But even the kindergarteners spent just a little time discussing before diving in. The key point is to come up with an initial plan of action so that you can implement and test it, much like the scientific method of testing an initial hypothesis. So, for ministry, this would mean opting for a quick, minimally-involved approach for reaching your target flock as you get going, then choosing *doing* outreach over *planning* it. As great entrepreneurs often say, failure is good! Learn from your mistakes and continue to get better.

2. **Implement** – This is the fun part where you get to see your plan in action! Again, do NOT be afraid of failure. This is what holds many people back. They get overly discouraged when just a few people show up the first time, or their first video on social media only gets a few views. They think: Was it the time of day? Was it the way I promoted it? These are good questions to ask, but don't let them paralyze you while the outreach is happening! Execute your first outreach, and above all, do not close up shop just yet! Many people let just one or two failures set them back. Don't do this. Implement, then go to the next step.

3. **Observe** – This is where you look back at your

outreach and evaluate its successes and failures. Again, much like the scientific method, look back at your outcome, then consider all the variables you can adjust. Was outreach less than expected? Why might that be? If you believe it is the day/ time, then adjust this variable for the next outreach. If it may have been the theme or marketing materials, adjust those and see what happens next time. Did you have an awesome turnout and abundant fruit? If so, why did that happen? Focus on the key causes and turn up the gas for next time for even better results! While you shouldn't be afraid of failure, please also don't be afraid of success! This can stop people in their tracks too, thinking their catch was just too big. Fear not, God will help you address all the needs that surface—He did feed five thousand with just five loves and two fish. When thinking about what to work on for the next cycle, try to isolate down to one or two variables you want to change, then start the process all over again.

Perfect is the enemy of done, and we think this framework can give peace of mind to people who find themselves locked in the planning stage because they try to sort out every little detail. Remember, this is not your magnum opus and you can't boil the ocean. Another way of saying this is that good judgment comes from experience, but experience comes from bad judgment. If you want to be successful, you have to be willing to risk mistakes. There are simply not enough books and not enough time to read them all to know if everything you are doing is perfect. Work prudently and judiciously, then get out of your own way and make it happen.

Summary

The remainder of the book is divided into two sections: How Do We Get There and Where Next. If your outreach is coming up, we recommend that you read this book as if you were going through a training manual on how to successfully plan and execute. Alternatively, you could re-invent your ministry as you read along. Whichever you choose, please know that we are praying for you as we write this book. We have great trust that the Lord will bring about abundant fruit through your disciplined and sacrificial efforts to lay down your life for others, just as He did for you.

PART 1

How Do We Get There?

CHAPTER 3

GET A GRIP

I (Justin) remember that morning just like it was yesterday —sitting outside on the back patio of my home at sunrise while reflecting on my immense failures. The night before, no more than five teens had showed up at my youth ministry night, six months into the job! My tenure as youth ministry coordinator started with much enthusiasm, but attendance slowly dwindled from fifty to thirty to ten . . . and now five. Where had I gone wrong? What was I doing, or not doing, that was causing such dismal results? Why weren't kids coming to our gatherings?

Upon further reflection, I realized I didn't have a firm grip on my ministry. Most importantly, I had forgotten to focus on who I was trying to serve, rather than what made life easy for me and my programs. That day, I called the kids who stopped showing up, and invited them to our next event and pizza beforehand, just to listen to them, get to know them, and understand why they stopped participating. That was the beginning of the resurrection of the ministry.

Oftentimes in ministry, we don't truly have a firm grip when we set out. We either make the ministry about ourselves or have a fuzzy and unclear picture of what we're trying to accomplish. We vaguely say, "I want to help teens" or "I want to help men." That simply isn't a strong enough grip on the problem we're trying to solve or the people we want to reach. To aid us in having a firm grip on our ministry, we've created a framework called the **5 Ws**:

5 Ws

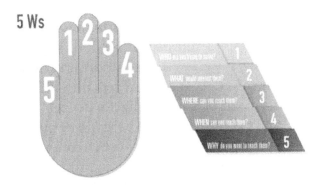

This framework is great to introduce and think through at the beginning of a brand new ministry. Think of it as structured brainstorming. And every so often, it's helpful to revisit even when your ministry is up and running to make sure your priorities are still correct. Let's dive in one-by-one.

WHO Are You Trying to Serve?

Who is the focal point of all of your outreach? Who are the people you want to see filling your events and engaging deeper in their relationship with Christ as a result of all that you do?

Now, simply being able to *name* who we are trying to serve isn't the same thing as actually *knowing* them. You should know their interests, hobbies, what type of media they use, and more. What is their prayer life like? What do they do for fun? What annoys them, etc.? There is only one way to get these answers—by spending time with them and listening to them. Here's both a bad and a good example of what I mean.

Bad: I am trying to serve teens, ages eleven through

eighteen.

Good: I am trying to serve middle school and high school youth, ages eleven through eighteen. They are roughly an even mix of public-school and private-school students, and they accurately represent the diversity of my community. They don't use Twitter anymore and they certainly aren't on Facebook. If I want to reach them on social media, I at least need to use the platform they are using (if permitted) and my posts need to be a mix of information and relational. They are not interested in going too deep in their faith just yet, but they are curious for more. So, I need to meet them where they are. They love to eat and they want food that is hot and fresh (not reheated casserole). Also, every event needs to be different and fresh; never do the same thing twice!

Do you see the difference? That bad example—that would've been me when I started my job in youth ministry. The good one was after a couple of years. How do you improve your answer? Simply getting to know who you are trying to serve! Spend time with them, eat lunch with them in the cafeteria, laugh with them. If you build a relationship first, then you will really have their attention *and* get to know them beyond the superficial. Knowing WHO you are serving, and constantly reminding yourself of who they are, is the first step towards making a map. More suggestions on how to get to know your target flock come a bit later in this chapter.

WHAT Would Interest Them?

If you've been able to provide an in-depth answer for WHO, this next one should come pretty easily. By knowing their likes and dislikes, interests, and pet peeves, you can tailor your programming and outreach to meet their needs. For example, based on my above description, would those teens like a Wednesday night session on different types of prayer or a game night where we teach Jesus's parables through sports in the gym? Hmm . . . don't ask me during my tenure as youth ministry coordinator. Yep, I would've been wrong. I tried that Wednesday night thing, and guess how many came? One. You know why? Because she felt bad and knew no one else was coming. But thankfully, we did the parable event soon after, and guess what? It was awesome. So, get to know your target audience well and then do things that interest them, not things you think they need. Meet their needs and then keep bringing them closer to Jesus at the pace that works for them.

WHERE Can You Reach Them?

With the gift of modern technology, this no longer has to be a physical place! Where are they spending their time? What is convenient for them?

Did you notice how I didn't ask what is convenient for *you*? So often we plan ministry around what's easiest for the volunteers, or the staff, or Father. We must ask ourselves: is this ministry about us or them? If we get that answer right, then we start to think about things correctly.

So, go to them. Make life easy for them. Jesus didn't say the Good Shepherd waited for the lost sheep to come back —He went to go find them. So, if your group is having trouble coming to a certain location . . . move it! Or, if they can't come at all, go to them. As long as we step into their shoes, we will get this question correct more often than not.

WHEN Can You Reach Them?

Now for the pinky: What day and time is convenient for

them? Back to my past failures for a second—another problem with my Wednesday night prayer event mentioned above? The teens were SUPER busy on Wednesdays! Why didn't I take the time to think of that? But Sunday for parable night? Perfect. The kids were already used to ministry on those evenings. The principle works here again—do what is helpful to your target audience.

Also, why limit your event to one time a week? The COVID-19 pandemic helped us see that some ministries can meet multiple times a week with great success. During the lockdown, we were invited to make a virtual presentation for a dynamic youth ministry. The youth minister organized three retreats during the first two months of lockdown and seemingly held online events every night of the week. What happened? The people who only had Tuesdays free were finally able to join the youth ministry!

There is a banking commercial with a tagline that goes something like, "You don't work bankers' hours . . . neither do we." If the people you are trying to reach have schedules that don't fit with yours, why not expand your schedule if you are able? If you only meet once a week, you automatically eliminate anyone with a variable schedule, like restaurant staff or first responders. If Sunday night meetings are a sacred cow, yet ineffective, it might be time to do things differently.

WHY Do You Want to Reach Them?

And now the thumb: You might be asking yourself, why is the thumb the last one? Well, because that finger helps you have a firm grip on your map. So, while it's last, it's actually the most important. Never forget your WHY. I'll say it again, never forget your WHY! If we ever lose sight of this, we can kiss our ministry goodbye. You are here to make disciples. If your ministry simply exists to provide people with a fun activity or make them feel good, they can find that just about anywhere! Why do you do what you do? If it's not to make disciples, change it up! Everything we do needs to be about fulfilling the Great Commission—whether it's helping youth, seniors, moms, dads, or whomever, the goal is to help them follow Jesus and get to Heaven.

How to Get to Know Your Audience

As we mentioned above, it is important to get to know your audience: what interests them, what do they love, and what do they loathe, etc.? Here are several approaches that anyone can take to move in this direction. The key to making all of them successful is *listening*. If you ask questions just to validate your own approach, that doesn't count. While listening, you may hear something challenging about why people don't show up to your events or watch your videos, but the truth will set you free ... to improve!

Break Bread with Them

We know a famous street preacher and evangelist who did this pretty successfully—Jesus ("Why does your teacher eat with tax collectors and sinners?" - Matt 9:11). Sitting down to a meal with someone, whether for a fast-food burger or a fancy dinner, levels the playing field and does something special. Neither of us knows enough about psychology to say why this helps people feel more comfortable, but we know from experience it does. This may even require jumping in the car or on the train, but this is time well spent and it will tell you more about what people need than any book, blog post, or video ever could.

We have had many insightful meals at cafeteria lunch-room tables that were too small for us, or on street corners with the homeless for whom we had just bought coffee. People who were strangers just a few minutes prior opened up about not believing in God or struggling with belief because of the apparent hypocrisy of Christians. Some even told us candidly but with no malice that they thought the Church was lame, or that they wanted to get connected to God but didn't know where to start.

Eating together breaks down barriers and makes people feel comfortable. Perhaps one of the special things about it is that it puts almost everyone eye-to-eye. Breaking bread changes power dynamics, somehow reminding us of our common bonds rather than our differences—we all need to eat, right? It also provides natural opportunities for each to take turns. It's kind of like the old saying about pipes—they give a wise man time to think and a fool something to close his mouth on.

As tempting as it can be to eat with your peers (we never really outgrow primary school, do we?), this means that you should intentionally sit with your target flock whenever you can. If they do show up to an event, make it a point to sit with them and authentically listen to everything they have to say. If it isn't natural to ask about their interests or needs, wait until another time. You are still building trust with them, and this is actually more important than just knowing about how to minister to them. If you are a natural introvert, the hard part might be actually sitting down, while the listening will come easy. On the other hand, we extroverts need to remember to bite our tongue and listen *more* than we talk.

Digital Contact

Without a doubt, the people whom you are seeking spend some time online and you can find them, or at least the demographic group. For instance, did you know there are groups on social media dedicated to young Catholic working moms? Yes, as a matter of fact, there are. You will need to follow certain protocols and it may take a little bit of time to learn the rules of engagement (when you can post, what you can post about), but venturing into these places to get answers to the 5 Ws can be very helpful.

Don't forget phone calls either! These can be a big investment in time, but that comes with its own ROI. Giving people your time and showing genuine interest are foundational to friendship, and that is even more valuable to your ministry than learning about someone.

Coffee Chats

A middle ground between digital contact and breaking bread is to ask people out for coffee, tea, or whatever you think they would say yes to. This may fit better with someone's schedule than going to lunch or dinner, and may also feel like less of a demand on their resources. These meetups can be quicker, less expensive, and more casual. Your guest can also excuse himself at any time because he isn't waiting for food or the check.

What to Ask?

Sitting down across from someone, virtually or in person, is half of the equation, while the second is what to ask. First, let's return to the most important thing you can do —listen. Listening well is more important than asking perfect questions and even than getting helpful answers. Your ministry has already started and you are sowing the seeds for what you really want—discipleship. Yes, this person can tell you what people like him really want. But you don't want people in general; you want a person, an individual, and now he is sitting right in front of you! Treat him as if he will become the next cornerstone of your discipleship team. Maybe he will one day!

Here are some sample questions you could ask someone in an initial conversation:

1. Tell me your story: Who are you, and what's your background?
2. What are you interested in and what makes you laugh?
3. How is the Church serving you? What could the Church do better?
4. What are some ways you try to grow your relationship with God?
5. What questions do you have about the Church? Or challenges, or frustrations?
6. What would you be interested in learning more about, or trying to do, in order to grow in your relationship with God?

The key is to make it a conversation, not an interrogation. Remember that you need to be open, too! If you build a relationship, over time the more difficult and serious questions can come.

Surveys

The final suggestion we have is to create surveys. Nothing gets you more information in a timely manner, but we still recommend that you put plenty of time into them. Write the questions very thoughtfully to make sure that the answers give you what you really want . . . and then pilot the survey so testers can tell you if the questions are clear.

Surveys can seem impersonal and often are, so we hope that you don't only gather information via surveys. Maybe they are just a first step and you include an invitation to meet for coffee at the end. We discuss what goes into making a strong survey in Chapter 7 and we include sample survey questions in Appendix A.

So, with that, you have a firm grip ready for your map. Now it's time to actually create it.

CHAPTER 4

MAKE A MAP

Ever tried to get somewhere with a bad map, or without one at all? I (Justin) tried to accomplish this very feat once when my friends and I decided to visit one of our high school buddies at his college. Problem was, I entered the wrong address in the GPS and didn't realize it until over halfway through the trip! Thankfully, we found a gas station where a seasoned veteran of the roads was able to show us the route to our friend. He patiently walked us through the rest of our journey on a map we purchased. Due to poor planning, our journey took twice as long as it should have, but thankfully a good map helped us get back on track.

This story illustrates well the importance of having a good map from the beginning of a trip. Without it, we can easily veer off course, wind up at the wrong destination, or waste a lot of time. A map for your ministry can come in the form of a simple **Ministry Plan**.

It looks simple, but it can become more robust over time as your ministry grows and expands. No matter if your ministry is one-day old, or one-decade old, you should have one of these, and everyone on your team should know where to find it. The answers flow based on the 5 Ws we discussed in the previous chapter. Let's walk through the sections of the plan, and then we'll show you an example.

Ministry Plan

Purpose	Why does your ministry exist?
Vision	What do you want to see as a result of your ministry?
Name	What will everyone call your ministry?
Priority Areas w/ Goals	Which areas are key and what are some specific goals for each?
Plan	How will you start your ministry? What are you going to do and when?

Purpose: Why Does Your Ministry Exist?

Again, it needs to be connected to the Church's greater mission of making disciples. Is it to bring about healing in some way? Helping to form people in the faith? Building a stronger sense of Christian community? Whatever it is, as long as it is helping people truly live as disciples, it's in line with the Church's greater mission. Also, be explicit, not generic. For example, a strong purpose statement would say, "Help recovering addicts ages eighteen to twenty-nine grow as disciples of Christ, empowered to share their testimony and spread the Gospel for the rest of their lives." A poor one that is less explicit would look something like, "Help addicts follow Jesus." The more focused your mission is, the better.

You might say to yourself, "Do I really have to write this down?" YES. Don't trust yourself to just have it in your head. A clearly written purpose statement is vital not only to help keep you on track, but also to form and lead a team (coming in the next chapter). Everyone needs to know where he or she is going on this journey.

Imagine a room full of adult men, all committed to their faith, gathering early one weekday morning to come together and start a diocesan men's ministry. How many opinions do you think you will encounter about the best way to move forward? Probably at least one more than the total present!

The most important thing to do was get all of these men on the same page so the months ahead wouldn't be filled with arguments. Many of these men were professionals, others retired military personnel who had been accustomed to responsibility and authority, and others still were men who had been passionate about their faith for years and were convinced they knew what God wanted them to do. Out came the ministry plan framework.

Ryan, the only diocesan staff person present, was able to use this as a starting point and to help communicate with clarity to the men that they needed a singular goal. They might not agree on that presently, but the objective of that first meeting was to get their ideas out and on paper. It helped that the ministry already had the refining oversight of both the universal Church and the mission of the local Bishop, so the men simply had to share what they thought was important and Ryan only needed to referee, keeping things on track and trying to balance the conversation.

At one rather heated moment, one of the men, Jose, pounded the table as he exclaimed, "It has to get more men to adoration! People need to be able to come to the Lord and know He is real, He is really there!" Stephen, another member who was a little quiet but clearly someone who had thought a lot on the subject, had been explaining about the need for discipleship, the intentional process of establishing trust, sharing the story of Jesus, and eventually inviting someone to become a fully committed follower of Jesus Christ.

Ryan stepped in, "It can be both, guys. Jose, you are right; it does need to be about Jesus. But Stephen is saying the same thing. You love adoration and want other people to experience it like you do. Stephen wants people to have an encounter with the Lord. Both of you have important points, and they both belong to the mission.

In the end, the group settled on a mission statement that identified intentional discipleship as the most important goal of the ministry. The men also made sure to include Eucharistic language, recognizing the Eucharist as the source and summit of our life, and a powerful opportunity for an encounter with the Risen Lord.

Vision: What Do You Want to See Happen as a Result of Your Ministry?

Think of this as the mountaintop. When you've arrived, what will everything look like? Don't overthink it and be sure to dream big! And again, be explicit, but a vision is a bit different than a purpose statement. A vision is more what you want to see happening in five, ten, or even twenty years as a result of your ministry. If you were trying to develop a vision for a parish youth ministry, something like the following would be strong: "Our vision is teens on fire with the Catholic faith all across our parish and local neighborhoods, and graduates living lives of discipleship across the state." Your vision should be so big that it gets people excited when they read it and motivates them to get on board! They should look at it and say, "Yes! I want to be a part of that!"

Ryan knew that this step in the process would be more challenging. The mission statement wasn't too hard because he had big-picture people on the planning committee, but making that mission incarnate in the world would be tough. How could he get them to think concretely?

"I'd like to try something," Ryan started. "We all agree it won't be enough, in fact, it would be a failure, to have a great mission statement but not have a clear idea of the results we want. Can each of you take sixty seconds and describe this: If a man joins our ministry and becomes a fully committed Catholic, husband, and dad, what does his life look like?"

After the time had elapsed, Ryan waited for a volunteer. Jose waited a second and then chimed in, "He has to take his family to church every Sunday, to confession every Saturday, and go to adoration with them at least once a week."

Viet, a younger man whose faith had been strengthened because of a strong campus ministry in college, added, "He needs to be committed to sharing the faith and inviting at least one person into the Church a year."

"Why just one?" Joseph quipped, half in jest and half in earnest. Joseph, ever competitive, was Viet's best friend. "One seems like a lame goal."

The mood was light and fun, much less tense than it had been during the mission-planning process. "Well Joseph," started Ryan, "what do you propose as a non-lame goal? And just how many people did you invite to consider Catholicism in the last twelve months?"

"I can't remember," Joseph sheepishly admitted after a reflective pause. "But I know the ministry needs some form of *fellowship. Working out together, going bowling, eating barbeque, just something to get guys coming. If they don't think it is fun, they won't want to come."*

Ryan liked each of these three offerings and also believed that if men learned more about their faith they would only come to love it—and the Lord—more. The team settled on this vision of what they want to see twenty years down the road in their diocese as a result of their ministry: "Men on fire with the Catholic faith all across the diocese, leading their families and communities closer to Christ through prayer, service, and fellowship." As Ryan had stated earlier during the meeting, "A strong vision is both concrete and grandiose. It should also seem almost unattainable, but as Scripture says, "With God all things are possible" (Mt 19:26)

Name: What Do You Call Your Ministry?

You need a name that captures your purpose and clearly defines the ministry. Don't worry about being too creative or clever here. Simpler often works best. The most important thing? That when someone hears the name of your ministry, they understand what it's all about.

"How about Latin? Latin always sounds cool!", blurted out Joseph.

"But what if no one knows what it means?" responded Viet.

"I'm with Viet," Jose and Stephen both said, almost in unison. "The name should be something that everyone will understand right away and will tell people just what they need to know, nothing more," Jose finished.

"Catholic Men of the Rockies: Strengthening men and families through fellowship, faith, and service?" Ryan suggested. Not the most unique name in the world, but clear and concise enough that the rest of the men all agreed. They also thought

it would be fun for marketing and promoting the group—lots of great imagery of mountain climbing and reaching the summit could be used, relating back to their Eucharistic language and how our Catechism calls it "the source and summit of our faith" (CCC 1324). "I like it!" Jose added. "It is fun, and people will like talking about it!" As they closed, they all prayed his words would prove true.

Priority Areas with Goals

Given your target market (the WHO you are trying to serve) and the place you are taking them (your vision), you should be able to identify some priority areas (at least two or more). What is really going to move the needle for this group? Is it starting Bible studies? Some digital outreach? Social events to build community? Whatever they are, make sure they are something your flock will care about and will help move them towards the vision you've defined. Once you choose these areas, you should have one, two, or three SMART goals for each area. You might already know this, but SMART stands for Specific, Measurable, Attainable, Relevant, and Time-bound. Basically, you need goals that are clear, possible, and have a deadline. The worst thing would be to start a ministry without any goals at all, so at least write something to start! Is it attendance at events? Meals served by your outreach? Views on your social media videos? Whatever it is, start with something, and then it can evolve as your ministry starts growing and matures (more on that later in the book).

Ryan had an easy time with this one. Only ten percent of the parishes had an active men's ministry, and he knew that the first step was to increase that number. "How about after year one, we have twenty-five percent participation, followed by fifty percent in year two and sixty-two and a half percent in year three?"

"Those are good goals, Ryan, but participation alone won't be enough", replied Viet. "We need to make sure guys are actually becoming disciples, not just showing up and eating pizza. Can we also include goals about moving men from just sort of Catholic to devoted, and from devoted to disciple?"

"Sure", Ryan said, "but how do we make them SMART?"

Jose jumped in, "I got it! At some point, early in the ministry, let's do a quick survey whenever a new guy comes to find out how he describes His relationship with God, then again at the end of the year for everyone."

"That is a good start; it's specific and definitely relevant, but we need to be able to measure it and we need a goal to shoot for", Ryan added. "We still need a clear definition of the stages you are talking about, but how about we aim for twenty-five percent of men to move from the most basic stage up to the middle, and for ten percent to move from the middle to the highest level of commitment, by the start of summer when our ministry will take a break?"

Everyone agreed, and they moved on to planning.

Plan/Calendar

A plan/calendar is a simple outline of what you will do, based on the above categories. If you have goals, you certainly need a plan for how to reach them. Again, no need to be perfect here or overthink things. Start with something.

Below is an example of a completed ministry plan, based on the above story. As you can see, this plan is pretty lightweight and simple, something that is not cumbersome to carry around. Isn't that how a good map should be? Ever tried folding up one of those gigantic maps and putting it in the glove box of your car? That part is even more complicated than the journey itself! A good map is simple, easy-to-follow, and easy to share with others. It should require minimal explanation; someone else should be able to pick it up, see what your journey is all about, and how you plan on getting there.

Purpose	To serve men of the diocese, equipping them to be disciples that adore Our Lord in the Most Holy Eucharist.
Vision	Men on fire with the Catholic faith all across the diocese, leading their families and communities closer to Christ through prayer, service, and fellowship.
Name	Catholic Men of the Rockies Tagline: Strengthening men and families through fellowship, faith, and service
Priority Areas w/ Goals	1. Stimulate parish groups – increase percentage of parishes with men's groups from 10% to 25% after 1 year, 50% after year 2 and 62.5% after year 3. 2. Increased discipleship – 25% of men involved in parish groups move from basic to middle discipleship, and 10% to move from middle to high by summer, annually (based on survey data—exact descriptors of each level to be described in survey)
Plan	1. Host event for current and potential leaders of men's groups within the first 3 months. 2. Provide monthly training opportunities for group leaders starting in month 4. 3. Have weekly calls with individual parish leaders to provide ongoing support and resources starting in month 6.

What Do We Really Want to See?

In the narrative that followed the planning process, you may have noticed several themes in the ministry areas that the committee recommended: word, worship, fellowship, and sacrifice. These four areas are what we call the foundational Christian lifestyle and they come right from scripture:

In Acts 2:42-47, we read:

> They devoted themselves to the teaching of the apostles and to the communal life, to the breaking of the bread and to the prayers . . . All who believed were together and had all things

in common; they would sell their property and possessions and divide them among all according to each one's need. Every day they devoted themselves to meeting together in the temple area and to breaking bread in their homes. They ate their meals with exultation and sincerity of heart, praising God and enjoying favor with all the people. And every day the Lord added to their number those who were being saved.

The life of early Christians can be divided into four clear areas: word, worship, fellowship, and service. If it worked for them, why not for us? One of the clear benefits is that living this way sets your life apart; you truly become a light set on a lampstand and salt for the world as Jesus calls for (Matt 5:13-16). The early Christians lived differently than everyone else, so they looked different to everyone else.

This type of otherness arouses curiosity in non-Christians and is a great starting point for conversations with a non-Christian world. So, as you set goals and envision the future for your parish and fellow parishioners, we think these areas constitute the foundational Christian lifestyle and should be the organizational blueprint for everything you do. They will make your following more like Christ, and thereby make them more attractive icons of Christ to non-Christians.

This type of visioning also fits well with the third stage of the Flock Experience: envisioning the type of relationship we want to have with people, and the way of life we hope they adopt. As you set your goals, think back to what you know about your audience, especially about their needs and what they will attend. If they already participate in one of the word/worship/fellowship/service areas, maybe that is an easy place to start. Or, maybe their growth as Christians is stunted because they are imbalanced and only focus on one thing, not the whole of the Gospel. A balanced approach will ultimately draw them deeper into the heart of Christ.

Word	Worship	Fellowship	Service
Scripture	Mass	Barbecues	Job coaching
Church Fathers	Liturgy of the Hours	Saint Day Parties	Food pantry
Theology of the Body	Adoration	Bowling	Language classes
Social teaching	Praise and Worship	Family Movie Night	Resume advice
Catechism	Rosary	Seasonal Octave Celebrations	Habitat for Humanity

One last thing to remember—and a part of the Discipleship Funnel—is that we need to keep in mind the level of readiness of each person and group. If you are still casting a broad net, they might not want a study of the untranslated works of Thomas Aquinas. Or, if people are on the threshold of true discipleship, we don't need to host an event on how to find the Gospels in the Bible. If what you offer meets their needs, is appropriate for their stage of discipleship, and falls into one of the categories of word, worship, fellowship, and service, you will be in good company . . . the early Christians!

So, at this point, you've taken the time to really get a grip on your ministry through the 5 Ws. You also have a map showing you where you need to go and how you plan on getting there. Time to start the engine, right?

Not quite. You can't do this alone. You're going to need some help. Time to fill the car!

CHAPTER 5

FILL THE CAR

Is there a part of a road trip fuller of anticipation than filling the car? Think of your last long drive and of all the things you *thought* you needed—snacks for two months, a dozen audiobooks, a little *War and Peace* to page through while your friend takes the wheel, a suitcase big enough for every outfit you might wear, and the list goes on. But nothing was more important than who was in the car with you! The right companions made for a true adventure. This chapter is all about establishing the right team for the journey.

Team Charter

Our long-term plan is discipleship and your team is trying to get people there. The team charter is the starting point to make sure there is clarity and focus for everyone on the team, and available in a variety of ways. This framework helps you to establish and share a purpose, to name your ministry in a way that reminds you and your audience why you exist, to set and define job owners and responsibilities, and to establish *how* you want to be as a team. In addition, it lays out a plan for keeping essential information flowing so that you keep traveling at ludicrous speed.

Purpose	Why does your team exist?
Name	What will everyone call your team?
Members and Roles	Who are the members and what are their titles and roles?
Core Values	What core values will dictate everything you do and how you act?
Communication Plan	How will you communicate with each other? Meetings included.

Purpose

This is not the first nor last time we will discuss purpose; just keep in mind that team purpose needs to be situated within the overall purpose of creating disciples who make other disciples. This means knowing where your target audience is in the Discipleship Funnel. It also means thinking about Flock Experience. Jesus is unchanging and we don't need to doctor Him up for others to fall in love. Nonetheless, we can put ourselves in their shoes to try to understand how they need to hear the Gospel in order to be moved, and more importantly, how we can stay connected with them through the process.

Name

The name should remind both team members and your target flock of your purpose, at least if it's public. Otherwise, you are losing an opportunity to reinforce something essential to the group. You also run the risk of your team drifting away from the main goal as you move forward.

Members and Roles

How many people you need and what they do will be determined by your purpose. If you are lucky enough to hire someone, consider looking for the skillset that you need most (both on this team and any other initiatives you might undertake) *and* that is the hardest to find in co-workers and volunteers. Naturally, this will be different for everyone. We both feel comfortable speaking in public, so that wouldn't be a standout need. But neither of us know graphic design or video/audio editing. Those skills might be at the top of the list for new additions to the team, as would anything else that we thought could make the project more successful.

Clarity on Roles

One of our friends in grad school completed a dissertation on how infrequently principals created improvement plans for their *least efficient* teachers. Of the thousands of teachers at the bottom of the state efficiency rating, only a handful had a documented improvement plan. The researcher believed this was due to several factors. First, teachers were mostly agreeable people. Principals, having been drawn from the ranks of teachers, were also agreeable and unlikely to create conflict with their employees by setting clear steps for improvement. Who suffers when leaders can't have clear conversations on how to get better? The people we are trying to serve.

We have learned the hard way that if you are not clear

upfront, you will have much more difficult conversations with your team members further down the road. There are many, many ways to be clear about who is expected to do what, but one option is to make a complete list of jobs at the beginning of the team forming stage. Every job on the list should have an owner and everyone should know who owns what jobs and when the job should be complete. Afterward, compare the list. Does Ty have fifteen jobs, but Karen only has four? You know what to do. Ty will appreciate it, and Karen will too. It says that you respect Ty and trust Karen, and you will avoid any suspicion of favoritism!

Core Values: Your Touchstone

The idea of a touchstone was that you could take a substance harder than gold so that if you rubbed true gold on it, you would see a trace of the precious metal. This lets you know if the mineral you had in your hands was real gold and of what quality, or if it was just a shiny garbage stone. The touchstones of a team are your core values. These do for team initiatives what a touchstone does for gold: reveal true character.

Almost as soon as we undertook this project, we established core values for our partnership. It gave us touchstones against which we could test our efforts. Was a certain idea truly valuable to the project, or was it interesting and attractive but ultimately not helpful? By comparing the idea to our core values, we had a quick way of knowing what was critical and what wasn't.

The values we chose were prayerfulness, honesty, partnership, and personal holiness. Shortly thereafter, we added truth in charity. Why these? Honesty and partnership were among the first things we discussed to make

sure that we felt comfortable saying when we felt un-
comfortable. We set an expectation that each would treat
the other as an equal partner, as we would want to be
treated. Prayerfulness and personal holiness were the next
to come. Prayerfulness so we could discern everything in
this book. Personal holiness to remind us that if we are not
growing in our love for God while writing this book, fulfilling our vocation as husband and father, and showing fruit
in the apostolate that the Lord has appointed to us, then
we were not operating within His will and needed to pivot.

Having a book that built upon the best practices from
business and education was important to us, as we have
both grown tired of reading opinion-based critiques of the
Church. Instead, we wanted to focus high-impact strategies for what the Church really needs—moving the needle
and reversing the trend of disaffiliation. The realization
that our mission was urgent led to truth in charity. We
need to be clear and honest, but we must always be guided
by fraternal charity.

So, what are your core values? We suggest that you identify the one or two values from which all other values flow.
Personal holiness was an easy one for this, as we know that
the reason we are here is to know, love, and serve God (holiness). If we aren't getting that part right, what we are doing
is wrong, even if it has the semblance of virtue.

To identify your core values, check out the list of values
in Appendix B. We compiled this list based on common
leadership characteristics and traditional concepts associated with holiness. First, just go through and circle or high-
light everything that grabs your attention. Next, compare
the contents of the list and identify only those that are
most important (isolate) and least important (cross out)

to you.

If you still need help refining your values, ask some of these questions:

1. Which of these values keep you focused and motivated?
2. Against which do you already compare your ideas, decisions, and work to determine if they are the right stuff?
3. Upon which are your other choices based?
4. Which core values may seem like "common sense" to one team member, but helpful to have clearly stated for another?
5. What does our team need to be reminded of again and again?

Communication

If I have information that you need, it belongs to you. My job is to get it to you in a way you can understand. This is the heart of team communication. Sounds simple enough, yet poor communication plagues organizations big and small, rich and poor. Even the tragic disaster of the Space Shuttle Challenger was partly caused by a breakdown in communication.

Solving this problem has contributed to several library shelves worth of books, but here are some simple things you can do to head in the right direction. As you proceed, pay attention to where communication consistently breaks down. This will help you identify the areas of greatest need. As you might have guessed, start by making a plan and using support structures to help you stay on course. The big questions are when, who, what, and how.

When: How frequently do you need to check-in and

exchange information? Strong teams tend to over-communicate but do this in a concise way, not constantly dumping all of their thoughts on teammates. Constant contact through modern instant message platforms can work great, but they can also disrupt the concentration and focus needed for deep, productive, and creative work. We recommend no less than a once-a-week team check-in where members give an update about where they are in their tasks, any changes, and what information they still need, and from whom. This can be part of a regularly scheduled meeting, or it can be more informal using email or a messaging service.

Who: Which people have a right to the information that only you possess? Who is waiting to complete a job until they get the information only you have? Have you changed anything that would be helpful to someone else on your team? We recommend that you keep a list handy of everyone who may be affected by your decisions. I (Dan) failed to do this while planning a very large event that occurred while working on this book. I had scheduled speakers for the same workshop topic but in multiple languages. About three weeks before the event, I added an additional language track. Did I remember to tell everyone who needed to know? Nope. It wasn't until a meeting a week before the event that I brought it up. My poor communication created a lot of stress and extra work for others, and with a very limited window to finish it! Had I consulted my list, I would have remembered to communicate with the right people in a timely manner.

How/what: No matter what you use, every meeting should have dedicated time for open sharing of information. We don't recommend putting this at the end of a meeting, as running over in other areas may squeeze this out. Schedule it early on when people are still fresh and engaged, and as much as you can, encourage vulnerability. What do we mean by that? Vulnerability means that people need to feel comfortable sharing news even when it is not good. In other words, they trust you!

There are many ways to establish trust in your team (e.g., retreats, social outings, team building workshops), but one surefire way to destroy it is to correct, criticize, or ridicule people for their mistakes in a public setting. Here is a good rule to follow: Praise in public, correct in private. Anyone who would have been ashamed of correction before their peers will hopefully feel confident enough to admit failure or even just share disappointing news if they know you have their back.

There are many good programs out there to help you communicate easily and keep track of who owns a job, when that job is due, and who is waiting on information from someone else to move forward. To start with, we have a sample outreach checklist in a later chapter. As a team, you should decide which, if any, third-party program you want to use. Commit to updating this platform with all necessary information instead of keeping notes and ideas separately by everyone. This will visualize progress and keep communication in a central location.

Here is an example of a completed team charter for a ministry to senior citizens by senior citizens:

Purpose	To provide Christian community for seniors during the "golden years" of their lives, when they have more free time than they've had since they were children, and are eager to learn and serve.
Name	Guiders of the Golden Years
Members and Roles	Director – Provides overall vision and direction, has the final say on big decisions. Social Chair – Responsible for organizing social gatherings grounded in the faith, building fellowship. Service Chair – Organizes regular opportunities for members to reach out in service. Prayer Chair – Organizes prayer at all gatherings. Spiritual Advisor – Ensures the group is on track to emulate the attitudes and behaviors of the early Church.
Core Values	Evangelization – We exist to share Jesus with others. Commitment – We show up on time and complete our tasks. Empathy – We do our best to understand our target flock. Teamwork – We work together, not in silos. Fun – We make sure to have fun at every meeting and gathering.
Communication Plan	Daily text messages of encouragement/sharing ideas. Weekly phone calls to discuss upcoming initiatives. Monthly in-person meetings.

Conclusion

Having a successful team flows from having a clear purpose. After that, fill the car with passionate people who have the skills to help reach your destination. Everyone will have an assigned seat (someone has to be DJ, right?), which means that they own their jobs and are clear on their responsibilities and deadlines. As a team, establish core values to guide your interactions and work along the way. Last, decide when and how you will communicate with each other. If you do these things, you are in for a great trip with great people who feel secure and excited about their journey.

Do's and Don'ts

Do:

1. Clearly define your purpose.
2. Reinforce it in various ways (meeting openings, signs, email signatures, prayers).
3. Define core values together that guide your attitudes and behaviors.

4. Identify the skills, knowledge, and abilities needed and find teammates who fit those roles.

5. Communicate often but in a concise way.

Don't:

1. Try to boil the ocean! Your team has a clear purpose ... stick to it!

2. Have jobs without owners—make sure everything essential has an owner.

3. Think that you are being nice if you don't address failure. You are just being unkind to everyone else who is working hard!

CHAPTER 6

START DRIVING

I (Dan) love to cook and love hosting big gatherings of Catholic people. For me, it feels a bit like the early chapters of Acts of the Apostles. But earlier in life, I was a pretty stressed host. It all started in college with the Catholic Campus Ministry. My parents lived nearby, so anytime we needed a gathering for an Easter party, a bonfire, or just to get together, we would head on over to the Boyd Ranch, as it was affectionately called.

I always felt like I had to act as host, chef, pit master, tour guide, fire marshal (for the giant bonfires), and everything else. The problem was that I tended to forget things and become disorganized. One minute I would be peering into a dark, smoky grill to check the barbeque and the next I would be racing through a crowded house as I looked for cups, drinks, and serving utensils, all while smelling of smoke and sweat.

Eventually, it dawned on me that I wasn't actually having fun at my parties because I left too many details for the last minute. This led to frantic rushing to get things done. Of course, I inevitably forgot important things, like the expensive dessert in a cooler in my trunk. Did I eventually find out about those mistakes? Yes, but often much later than I would like to admit. A simple checklist would have solved most of my problems.

Start Driving!

Back to the road trip analogy. If you want to love the trip and have a blast hitting your milestones and making disciples, we want to introduce the next helpful tool: an outreach checklist. Using this as a starting point will make sure that you actually enjoy your outreach and don't get overstressed along the way!

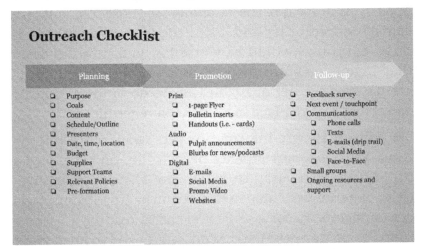

Outreach Checklist

Planning	Promotion	Follow-up
❏ Purpose	Print	❏ Feedback survey
❏ Goals	❏ 1-page Flyer	❏ Next event / touchpoint
❏ Content	❏ Bulletin inserts	❏ Communications
❏ Schedule/Outline	❏ Handouts (i.e. - cards)	❏ Phone calls
❏ Presenters	Audio	❏ Texts
❏ Date, time, location	❏ Pulpit announcements	❏ E-mails (drip trail)
❏ Budget	❏ Blurbs for news/podcasts	❏ Social Media
❏ Supplies	Digital	❏ Face-to-Face
❏ Support Teams	❏ E-mails	❏ Small groups
❏ Relevant Policies	❏ Social Media	❏ Ongoing resources and
❏ Pre-formation	❏ Promo Video	support
	❏ Websites	

Why, you may ask, is this simple tool so helpful? It's a little boring, you may say? Well, that's because the boring stuff is so easily overlooked but also crucially important. Ever run out of gas or need an oil change? Car maintenance is boring, but it's essential even for professional racecar drivers to win! This checklist contains a taste of what you will need in any successful ministry program. Let's take a look at the sample checklist above from left-to-right.

Planning

In the planning section, you always need to start with the purpose of the outreach and align it with your overall ministry purpose. You will also need some goals like attendance or some verifiable change in the participants. Of course, you need to think through the content, presenters, and logistics like day/time/facilities and budget.

One area that we find often gets overlooked is checking for compliance with important policies. Are you squared away with safe environment, speaker vetting, and social communications policies? You could have great execution but if you don't dot the I's and cross those T's, you risk damaging credibility and losing the trust of your leadership. Few things would be worse for your ministry than that! If you don't already have copies of the most important policies readily available, please do yourself a favor and print them to place in a quick reference file.

Additionally, pre-information gets away from us all the time. What do participants need to do, or have access to, prior to attending to make sure they have an awesome experience? This can range from having strong internet connectivity for a virtual event to reading a passage from Scripture or the Catechism beforehand to focus their thoughts. There is a lot you can do before the event to create a better experience for the flock.

Lastly, do not forget a practice run with your team! When you walk through the entire event before it actually takes place, make sure you've thought through every detail from the experience of your flock; you will realize instantly if you are missing something major. Picture yourself in their shoes—what do they see? What do they hear? Is check-in easy? How about leaving the event? What could improve the experience for them? Doing a mental and physical walkthrough will help to make sure you've covered all the details—and remember to do it from their vantage point and not your own. It's about them, after all!

On the checklists we use with our team, we have a section dedicated to the week-of and the day-of to ensure a thorough walkthrough. This may be redundant, but here is a story of why checklists can save your bacon.

In a previous ministry position, I (Dan) would do a mental walkthrough and stage supplies in the days leading up to large retreats. I stored music/audio equipment in a secure location, prepared conference handouts, then checked and double-checked waivers and medical forms. Once a year for a special retreat, I had to locate a locked box of senior letters, then would practically never let them out of my sight.

One of the biggest productions each year at the school where I worked was the senior retreat. A tradition that every senior looked forward to was opening the letter they wrote four years earlier on their freshman retreat. This was a note they penned to their future self. Sometimes, the note was heartfelt and contained hopeful dreams of what their four years in high school would hold: lettering on one or more varsity teams, going to prom with their best friends, or getting into their parents' alma mater. Other letters were a little less serious, and some even included whatever money the student happened to have in their pocket at the time.

No matter what the student wrote, the letter provided a window into the past and a snapshot of their transformation. What they found funny at fifteen, they had (hopefully) long since outgrown. This provided a great platform from which to discuss spiritual growth and to make commitments for their faith into their college years and beyond.

But what if we, the retreat team, forgot the letters? That

is why I had the checklist. Each year after the freshmen retreat, our team gathered all of the letters and put them in a locking, weatherproof container. On the outside I would write in bold, permanent marker, in all capital letters, "DO NOT THROW AWAY EVER – FRESHMAN LETTERS CLASS OF . . .". I then took this box and locked it behind not just one but two doors, and there they stayed for nearly four years until I looked over the checklist for the senior retreat.

Every year as we went through the checklist and performed our mental walkthrough, I would double-check the box to make sure it was still there. The night before the retreat I would finally move it, staging it with all of the other retreat supplies. Each step of the way, the checklist included a box to tick off and make sure I still had the letters. This may seem like overkill to some of you, but during my time at that school, I never once forgot the letters. At least I can say that part of the retreat was a success!

A friend who had held a similar position at a different school explained to me what happened one time when he forgot his senior letters. His retreat was more than an hour away from the school and after he had successfully loaded and unloaded over a hundred rowdy high school seniors and was about to begin their retreat, it struck him like a lightning bolt: he didn't have the letters! During the summer he had taken them home to make sure that they wouldn't accidentally be thrown away during the annual deep cleaning, but he had forgotten to bring them back to school. Handing the reins of the retreat to one of the chaperones and praying that she would be able to keep it together, he jumped in his car and sped back home. He didn't tell us how fast he drove, but he did say he made record time. As fast as he went though, we bet he had plenty of time to think about how much he wished he had used a checklist like this one!

Promotion

Yes, it gets a whole section to itself. After prayer, promotion is hands-down THE most important thing to success in ministry. We cannot emphasize this enough. So many times, people wonder why they didn't have a great turnout. Did you promote the right message, to the right people, at the right place, at the right time? If you wanted to attract young adults to a ministry kick-off barbecue, did you only announce it in the bulletin? And did you use clipart in the advertisement? Millennials grew up with those icons at their computers at school; they will swiftly identify it as "lame" if the promotional materials are not up-to-snuff.

This is why we've provided a few different sample channels for advertising in the example checklist. Consider using all of them, as each can provide more participants, but be sure to prioritize one or two depending on your target group. You should know them well from the 5 Ws, and be able to identify where you can get their attention, be it print, digital, or word-of-mouth. And make sure to give your promotion enough time! We recommend at least one month out for a small event, such as a one-time social, service project, or Bible study. For a mid-size event such as a group study over three to four weeks or a one-day workshop, we recommend at least two to three months. For a large event such as a weekend retreat or conference, give your target market at least three to four months to prepare and block off their schedule.

Branding and Marketing

You can maximize your promotional efforts with a little branding and marketing know-how. Effective branding comes down to two basic principles:

1. Choosing a brand image that *resonates* with your target flock
2. Reinforcing that brand image *consistently* in everything you do

Much like a person we want to have a friendship with, we choose brands we want to have a relationship with. They need to appeal to something we are looking for and be consistent in how they portray themselves. Think about the clothes you wear, the products you buy, the movies you watch. At some level, you chose these because they resonated with something you were looking for, and consistently portrayed the benefits and values you desired.

Let's tackle the first component: choosing a brand that resonates with your target flock. This all comes back to the 5 Ws. If you know your flock well and what they are looking for, you can create a brand that scratches that itch. This is known in the advertising world as "positioning." How do you want the "brand" of your ministry to be positioned within the mind of your target sheep? Are you fun and exciting? Are you mysterious and interesting? This should also align well with the core values of your ministry that we created previously. Another way to think of this is, if your brand were a person, what would that person look and sound like? Keep this in mind every time you make a social media post, print ad, or anything else that would re-emphasize your brand.

Now on to the second component: consistency. Here are some ways to establish this:

- A catchy name shown on all advertisements
- A consistent logo utilized in all channels
- Catchy titles for events that align with your overall ministry brand
- Taglines for your overall ministry and aligned out-reaches
- Repeatedly used, descriptive words for your outreach

For instance, if you were going to create a podcast for Catholic dads, you would want to develop a consistent look and sound—the same set of colors in your logo, your advertisements, and any associated graphics. Ideally, a logo and other branding efforts convey a clear message: What is the podcast about? What will they learn, Who is it for? This is the time to think about the 5 Ws.

When someone sees your branding, they shouldn't need additional steps to learn enough about you to decide to take the next step. They also should immediately recognize your brand when they see it. Any written or verbal descriptions of your podcasts and episodes should contain references to your mission and core values. Over time, this will ensure that your audience knows exactly what you are about so they can begin to expect a quality experience whenever they engage with you.

You don't need a team of marketing wizards or even a degree in marketing to find success in getting your message out there. It's less about creating that one perfect ad or spending a ton of money on the thirty-second Super Bowl spot than it is about being consistent, timely, and persistent.

Consistency also means sticking to your brand and not deviating. For each specific outreach, you don't need to attract everyone to be successful; you just need to attract that fraction of the flock you have in mind. If you are tempted to change your branding, go off message, or plan something that is not part of your core mission and values, don't!

In an astronomy class once, my (Dan's) professor attempted to answer the question, "What is the best way to keep a giant asteroid from colliding with earth?" His answer might surprise you. He explained that if you saw it coming far enough off, you could launch small satellites towards the asteroid that would pass just by one side rather than strike it. The gravitational pull of even those small objects could be enough to change the trajectory and keep the asteroid from colliding with our home.

If you are an astrophysicist and reading this book, please forgive me for any errors I made in this example, but it provides a helpful analogy for speaking about timely marketing. Attracting someone to your event is a bit like this process. Rather than trying to make one monumental effort just in the nick of time, if you make early and small efforts leading up to your outreach, you are more likely to move someone towards the desired result. The small but perceivable gravitational pull of your advertisements will gradually change their trajectory towards you.

For timeliness, err on the side of being early rather than late. Not sure whether to send the save-the-date out six months in advance or three? Go with six. After that, be consistent. Over time, your messages will have an impact and people will start to perceive the value in what you are offering.

Follow-up

Now we get to the most overlooked area in ministry. So

many times, we plan great outreach but don't think about follow-up until everything is over. This means we have to scramble to capture momentum, some of which is undoubtedly lost. In the worst case, it may simply be too late to implement any follow-up at all. For these reasons, you should go into the event with follow-up already planned.

For example, let's say you are organizing a women's conference with the goal of inspiring parish-based women's Bible studies. During the closing comments, you could invite attendees to sign up for a weekly leadership conference call so you can keep in touch and send out reminders. This way, the potential leaders can stay connected for encouragement and support as they get new groups started.

To take it a step further, you could set aside time the week after the event to call participants to see what they thought and how you can support them moving forward. To expand your reach, you could consider including your planning team in the follow-up and support. Team members could be paired with attendees for individual support, or if your team is ready, for a more formal discipleship process.

Your follow-up plan will work best if it aligns directly with the goals of the overall outreach *and* is feasible for your team. Update your team at planning meetings about the follow-up so that all involved know what to expect, especially after the main outreach is over. You would hate to lose all of your able-bodied helpers and have them fall off the radar once the harvest is ready! It's imperative to have your team committed through the follow-up activities, not just the event itself.

This Outreach Checklist we've provided is merely an example. You can tailor it to your specific outreaches. Just make sure to keep the essential and overarching categories of planning, promotion, and follow-up.

Don't forget follow-up! We repeat—don't forget follow-up! Having a checklist like this as you plan your initiatives can help you make sure nothing slips through the cracks. If, every time you plan, you sit down and try to come up with all of these things anew, you will likely forget something. Take your checklist out every time you start a new idea, just to make sure all your bases are covered.

Now that we've discussed how to make sure every ministry outreach goes off without a hitch, let's focus on how to make sure everything we do is helping us achieve our larger purpose and reach the intended destination of our journey. Stay on course!

CHAPTER 7

STAY ON COURSE

When an annual review is due, how do people know they deserve a raise? How does their boss know whether to praise, correct, or dismiss them? When you leave your ministry, how will you recognize success? One answer is **goals**.

Goals help us to know that we are doing what we said we would do. Whenever we start something, we should understand why we are doing it, and that is a simple way of defining our goals. If you were to go to work for someone and your boss could not tell you what you were supposed to do, or what success looks like, or how you would be evaluated, those would be huge warning signs. They might even be reason enough for not accepting the job!

Goals help us know what we should be doing, and just as importantly, they help orient and keep us on track while we are in the thick of it. Goals, when they are used correctly, help ensure we stay on course. But how do we use them effectively?

Quite simply, you should have regular check-ins, individually or as a team, referring to your goals and honestly assessing your progress. The magic is not in having the goals, but in actually referring to them and using them as guideposts. For many of us, this might be hard; we might be afraid of goals! After all, goals keep us accountable. With goals, we can no longer say, "Well, at least we tried." Or, "I'm sure it's making an impact; we're planting seeds." No! With goals, we have a mark to hit, and we get to see if we hit it or not.

But we need not be afraid of failure, for it represents an opportunity to learn. We get to ask why we didn't reach the goal, then adjust for next time. Let's commit right now to confronting any fear, checking those goals, and allowing ourselves to focus on our destination. As you put together your plan, be sure you schedule regular meetings to measure your progress. If that measurement tells you something good, celebrate! If it doesn't, reorient and re-prioritize so you get closer to the finish line. The next time you check your progress, you *will* have something to celebrate!

How to Use Goals Well

Creating goals that are really helpful, especially for staying on course, includes setting deadlines, establishing ownership and accountability, and being very clear about what you actually want. Deadline settings simply means that you divide a larger goal up into smaller, manageable, bite-sized pieces that you can more realistically tackle during the time you have scheduled between check-ins. Ownership means there are no unclaimed goals—every goal, or every part of a goal, has someone looking after it to make sure it grows up and becomes what it was meant to be. For example, Dan agrees to write this part of the book while Justin agrees to work on this framework. Without someone dedicated to each, your goals never become reality, because something that is everybody's job is actually nobody's job.

Breaking up goals into smaller ones also helps for those that might seem impossible to obtain. A goal achieved lets us know we are making progress, and the momentum from accomplishing bite-sized pieces of a larger goal propels you forward even faster. For instance, when I (Dan) was writing my dissertation, it took over a year to complete the manuscript, yet I still had regular goals to accomplish. The goals were negotiated between my advisor and me, and I knew that each step in the process opened one more door in a series of doors that would eventually lead to the conferral of a doctoral degree. But for this to work, I actually had to believe that each step along the way would bring me closer to the goal, rather than being just one more arbitrary hoop.

Ultimately, I came to see the goals like mile markers indicating that I was getting closer to completion. So it must be with our goals—they can't be the enemy; they must be our friend, a welcome reminder that we are headed in the right direction. When we choose not to work towards these goals, we are deciding to go somewhere else. Had that been my choice on the dissertation, that would have meant that I was choosing a destination other than a doctoral degree. With the goals we set for our team, your team chooses if they want to do them. If they don't, that means they are choosing a different direction and outcome. Accountability means that we tell people when their choices don't align with team goals.

Some of what we have described above are components of SMART goals. Besides a buzzword, what are SMART goals? We define them as specific, measurable, attainable, relevant, and time-bound targets that you set for yourself to keep you on track.

Specific means they are clear and simple enough to eliminate ambiguity about what is required. For instance, if you want to start a ministry for widows & widowers, your goals should measure desirable outcomes with respect to members of that group. Other people may benefit, but you can't define the success of that ministry based on a different group of people.

Measurable and attainable go hand-in-hand, and the classic example of a goal that is neither measurable nor attainable goes something like this: we are going to get as many people as possible to attend our event. What's wrong with this? For one, that is not a number you can ever reach. "As many as possible" is so unclear that it is meaningless. Does that mean every active parishioner, every human being in the parish boundaries, every American, etc.? And it will always have been possible to attract more people than you did, and your supervisor will always be able to point to this. "Oh, fifty people showed up? Why wasn't it sixty, or one hundred?"

To be measurable and attainable, you need a finite number that you can compare with your actual results, and it should be a number that you can have reasonable confidence in attaining. Do you want to host a conference with ten thousand attendees but your local population is only twelve thousand? Is your conference just for men? Getting to ten thousand is not going to happen!

Once you have a specific, measurable, and attainable goal, then the next questions to ask are if the goal is relevant and time-bound. Relevant: is the result you hope to produce related to your ministry purpose? For instance, let's say you wanted to use a survey to measure some aspect of conversion and repentance in students. Your survey questions would need to be about things like their desire to go to confession, their willingness to go on their own, their willingness to attend if a priest were available at that instant, etc., and definitely *not* questions about content and knowledge of the sacraments. This is assuming, of course, that this outcome is in line with your ministry purpose and vision.

Time-bound means that you have a deadline—you want your men's conference to happen on March 28 this year, not at some distant point in the future. Until you have a deadline, you won't know how much you need to get done within a certain timeframe, which in turn keeps you from dividing your big goal into smaller, more manageable goals.

Think of SMART goals like bumpers on a bowling alley —they keep your ball going in the right directions and out of the gutter. By specifying what you want and making it measurable and attainable, you can know that your ministry is producing results. By keeping goals relevant and time-bound, you ensure that your efforts produce the results you want, when you want them. The deadline also allows you to divide the remaining work into manageable chunks so you can budget time each week, or between check-ins, so that you don't have to move heaven and earth in the last few days before your outreach.

What Do You Want to Know?

Broadly speaking, in ministry we want to know that we reach the right *people* and that we facilitate the right *change*. The first is really about attendance and participation, while the latter is about conversion. Numbers are important, but only if we see the spiritual fruit that we want. Measuring conversion might seem like measuring a cloud, but there are ways to measure if someone is turning to God.

Focusing on numbers alone seems to cause much-wasted effort in ministry. Events that attract large groups but do not facilitate lasting change are expensive and ultimately a waste of time. Getting people in the pews is a necessary step, but it is never the final goal. We also need to wrestle with the reality that Jesus's ministry did not focus on large groups, even though he does hold the record for World's Largest Fish Fry. He invested heavily in a small group so that he could produce good fruit that lasted a lifetime.

Getting Them in the Door

Having people show up tells you a lot: the price was right, people hungered for what you offered, you got the word out, and the timing was good. But, actually, these are goals you should assess during the planning process, not just after the event. This will help you maximize success. If you aren't hitting your benchmarks, there is still time to change things like frequency and type of advertising. Other elements, like price, are a bit harder to change, but you might still be able to make adjustments before it's too late.

For example, let's say you are the campus minister at a large Catholic high school. You have had success with a women's retreat and now want to try for a men's retreat. After establishing how many people you *need* to attend to meet financial goals, you then ask, *"How many am I likely to get?"* Hopefully the answer to the first question is smaller than the answer to the second; otherwise, you might consider another way to connect with those high school boys.

Next, set benchmark registration numbers at certain intervals leading up to the retreat. If you want forty guys to attend, then you might decide you want five people registered four weeks out, ten at three weeks, twenty-five at two weeks, thirty-five at one week, and forty the final week. Great, we ticked all the boxes for SMART goals!

Now what happens if you don't hit these numbers? Start asking questions, and the answers to these questions will tell you what to do. Is the price wrong? Offer scholarships, and if you know some people would like to attend but don't have the money, offer to reduce the fee. Are they interested and do they even know about it? Did you contact their parents or just hope that the flyer would magically pull itself out of the backpack and appear unwrinkled in mom's hands?

Your retreat meets a spiritual need, but are they aware of that need, and do they even know about the retreat? If not, let's ramp up marketing and get out there and talk to people. When you ask questions and take the answers seriously, you learn what people really think and what these high school boys really want. If there is still time, change the event and the marketing to meet their desires. Email the parents more, mail home a flyer, run a Facebook ad, etc. Even if you can't change the marketing, you can try to help the students see how the retreat already offers something they want!

Maybe the initiative you are working on is not a one-time event but a series. This could mean trying to increase participation at Mass or lead a small group over several months. For these events, the questions stay the same but you have the good fortune of knowing that more people can show up next week and the weeks after, so you still have time to make critical changes.

Spiritual Change

Our soul is what makes us like God—we have an intellect and we have a will. The intellect knows and understands things and the will moves us toward those things. One of the simplest definitions of conversion we can think of is that we (or our wills) are moved to do things that we didn't want to do before: pray, go to Mass, learn more about God, love our neighbor, and spend time with other passionate Catholics. As we discussed earlier in the book, this is also a pretty good biblical basis for what it looks like to be a Christian, based on Acts 2:43-47: we worship, we fellowship, we serve, and we study the faith.

This description of early Christian life in Acts was a different-enough way of living that it made non-Christians pay attention, so why not look for it in our flock. Do they want to live differently as a result of what we are doing? Another way to conceptualize it is obligatory versus voluntary signs of faith: they have to go to Mass, but they don't have to do things like learn more about God, visit those in prison, or spend extra time in prayer.

We should consider adding goals that reflect these types of changes, and we don't have to wait until the end of our initiative. For example, for members of a discipleship group, we can check in about various forms of internal, spiritual change, measured over time. Asking every week might be tiresome for you and them, but every other week or once a month would allow time for the Holy Spirit to work and account for variations in their mood.

Some other attributes of spiritual change that you can attempt to measure include:

- Shifts in disposition/emotions:
    - Are they happier or more joyful?
    - Do they experience greater hope than in the

recent past?
- ◦ Are negative emotions, such as depression or anger, subsiding?
- Inclinations and desires to do good:
  - ◦ How likely are you to _____? You can fill in the blank here with any number of expressions of a lively faith: attend daily Mass or adoration, go to confession, join a small group, talk to a stranger about your faith, raise your children Catholic, or consider embracing the Church's teaching on contraception.

It's worth noting here that emotions and feelings have been beat up a bit in discussions about authentic holiness. "It's not all about feelings, you need the CROSS!" or some variant thereof is a common objection when someone suggests measuring changes in inclination and disposition. Nonetheless, the language of the scripture is heavily emotional and it is only through our body, senses, and emotions that we experience God. From this point of view, measuring emotions is indeed Biblical.

As odd as it may sound, there are physical changes that signal conversion: time and place. **Where** people spend their time and **how** they use it are clear indications of what is important to them. The same holds for their finances. Asking questions about changes in these types of behavior can yield important details about your goals. Are your small group participants choosing to spend their time or money in less secular (or less sinful) ways? If there is no measurable change, it doesn't mean nothing is happening, but it might mean that your approach is not high-impact/high-yield. Consider if that is what you want.

How to Ask Questions and Collect Information

Before we jump into the details, we want to say that you don't always need to use surveys and questionnaires. Instead, take advantage of casual conversations, phone calls, and any communication. Listen well and keep a record of peoples' spiritual growth. Have they grown in trust? Are they more curious about the faith? If you really listen and ask some clarifying questions, people will share their spiritual journey with you in greater detail than you could ever capture in a survey.

While we love passive data collection, surveys and interviews are still valid and shouldn't be excluded from your repertoire. These can be formal—like a before/after survey that is emailed out—or informal. A good example of an informal survey is the kiosk in some airport terminals after you go through the security screening. The ones we have seen have two buttons: a smiley face and a sad face. The formal variety can give you more detailed information, whereas the informal type can give you greater overall participation, which is an example of the tradeoff paradox of surveys. The easier you make it, the more people will take it, but the less clear, actionable information you are likely to gather. Here is a summary of things to keep in mind when designing surveys and interviews:

- Delivery Format
  - Paper or online – higher response rate (paper) vs. convenient, inexpensive delivery (online): are you okay getting a lower response rate if you can easily deliver the survey to a thousand people?
  - Digital surveys can be done during an event just as easily as a paper survey can. Consider a QR or access-code-based survey to allow

people to finish a survey on their phone. These can give real-time information so you can adjust course *mid-presentation!*

- Delivery Time
  - Pre- and Post- are very valuable, especially if you measure individual changes.
  - When possible, put surveys in respondents' hands and be sure to give them a pen; ask for and collect them before people leave.
- Gathering Data
  - Some surveys you can just scan with your phone—no need to type in all that data! You can easily scan a template answer sheet and the app will gather and compile the data for you. You can also print basic QR codes to gather feedback *during* a presentation by asking people to hold up one of several codes to indicate their answer.
  - Consider using a service that offers basic statistical analysis—numbers tell a story but aren't always easy to follow!
- Precision
  - Align your questions with your goals: are your questions going to tell you what you need to know about success, or will they just add noise and chatter?
  - If people will answer a longer survey, ask the same question multiple ways; this can eliminate bias and correct for confusing questions.
  - Pilot the test ahead of time! Have multiple people take it and try to break it! Your questions may sound great in your head, but will

they make sense to others?

- ◦ Vary the question type: some multiple-choice, some scale (i.e.: very likely to very unlikely), binary (yes/no), some free-response.

- Length
  - ◦ The longer the event or activity, the longer your survey can be. An hour-long virtual prayer meeting doesn't need a ten-minute survey, but an all-day or weekend conference might!

- Frequency
  - ◦ I know this sounds like we are speaking out of both sides of our mouth, but people will get tired if you survey them too frequently—be judicious or your results will be skewed and your participation low.

Should You Change Direction?

Both Justin's dad and Dan's dad like golf, so this story is not incriminating. One of these golfers has a thing about never shooting over a hundred. No matter what, he *modifies* his score to make sure he doesn't feel too bad about his round. If we follow the planning process, we shouldn't need to change our destination mid-journey. However, some things are out of our control and there may be a good reason for changing the endpoint, thus reorienting all of your goals. What might this look like?

Perhaps you were planning a men's conference and then a one-hundred-year pandemic hits the world and you had to change your event. Maybe you keep a similar goal but you acknowledge that the format has changed, so you adjust your expectations. Or maybe you change the goal radically. Instead of increased participation in parish life, maybe you work towards helping men lead their families in prayer. Alternatively, maybe you thought you were meeting an authentic need but as you get closer to the event you realize that your target audience needs something very different. If it is not too late to change course without sacrificing quality, do it!

Just be honest with yourself and your team about changing goals before the journey is over. Here are a few questions to ask yourself:

- *Am I changing a goal because of external circumstances I can't control? Is there new information that forces me to pivot in order to truly reach my target flock?*
- *Am I changing this goal because it was too hard and I want an easy goal? Do I want to stay comfortable rather than pushing towards what is truly remarkable?*

The answers to these questions are everything—in fact, they are at the core of this book! If we fall into the temptation of always lowering the bar until we reach it, we won't make many disciples!

Staying on Course Dos and Don'ts

Do:

1. Treat goals as signposts (not "threats") that YOU establish to let you know that you are getting the RESULTS you want.
2. Schedule regular check-ins with your team to look for signposts; if you don't see them, you are not on course and won't get to your destination!

3. Assign an owner and a deadline to every goal.
4. Use SMART goals: Specific, Measurable, Attainable, Relevant, and Time-bound.

Don't:

1. Be afraid of your goals!
2. Assume that people will keep track of goals without scheduled check-ins.
3. Abandon your goals. If it is everyone's job, it is no one's job.
4. Create idealistic goals that sound nice but are impossible to capture.

PART 2

Where to Next?

CHAPTER 8

REARVIEW MIRROR

Isn't it satisfying to reach the end of a journey? This chapter is all about what to do when we've reached our destination. We can pull out the ministry plan, see the goals, and say, "Yep, we did it!" Our Lord would look at us and say, "Well done my good and faithful servant." We got a grip on our ministry, made a plan, put a team around us to make it happen, started driving, and kept on course until the journey was complete.

Well ... ***now what***?

This visual can show what our ministry journey may have looked like - we call it the **Ministry Life Cycle**:

Ministry Life Cycle

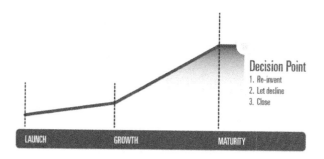

Decision Point
1. Re-invent
2. Let decline
3. Close

LAUNCH   GROWTH   MATURITY

1. **Launch**: This is when your ministry was getting started. It may have taken some time to get through this phase as you figured out how to work

with your team. You may have needed to adjust your plan and probably encountered some challenges. But after time, dedication, and hard work you moved to phase 2.

2. **Growth**: Your ministry really started to take off! You began to make progress on your goals and check them off. People began to talk more about your ministry, and there really was a "buzz" around it. This is often the most exciting part of ministry—when we actually get to see the fruits of our labor.

3. **Maturity**: Next, your ministry really started to round out and become a mature, disciple-making ministry, likely becoming a staple in your diocese or parish community. People know what is expected of your ministry and the kinds of results it produces. Time and time again, people keep showing up, and you keep reaching your goals. It almost feels like it will last forever! But be careful, the next phase might be around the corner.

4. **Decline:** Your ministry has started to decline. Attendance is hurting and you're not getting the results you want. You may be thinking, "Where did I go wrong? What's happened to my ministry? Is it no longer relevant?" First, don't worry. This phase is normal for all ministries. You can't produce amazing results forever and you may just need a little adjustment. But, the answer may be yes —your ministry might be irrelevant. Now is the time to ask yourself, "Is this still needed?" Once you've reached this phase, you've arrived at a decision point where you need to discern the future of the ministry.

Think of how the disciples must've felt when Jesus told them to lower their nets to the other side of the boat in Luke 5. When they pulled up their enormous haul of fish, surely, they were ecstatic! But after this, Our Lord told them to then drop their nets and follow Him—right after they made their biggest catch! Perhaps we need a similar attitude to our ministry—once our mission has been fulfilled, it may be time to let go and move on to something else, or hand it off to a different leader God has equipped for the job. This is why St. Ignatius of Loyola encourages us to have a spirit of detachment in all things, for we never know when it might be time to let go. Let's discuss what to do when you find yourself at this decision point. You have three options: (1) re-invent, (2) let decline, or (3) close.

The first option is to stay in the fight—to keep moving but take a fresh look at your ministry and adapt your approach. We've seen this in the business world with companies like Coca-Cola who have defied the odds and lasted much longer than most companies. How do they do it? They keep reinventing themselves. This juggernaut no longer considers themselves just a manufacturer of Coca-Cola, but a beverage company with a myriad of options. So, when trends set in that folks wanted less sugary drinks, they began to offer other alternatives. Now, they offer a variety of options and you may be surprised to find out which drinks are actually made by this company.

So, if you decide you want to keep your ministry alive and that it can still reach more people for Christ, where do you start in your reinvention? Jump back to the beginning of this book and answer the 5 Ws again. If the answers point to your ministry continuing, then keep pursuing it. What likely needs an adjustment is one of the next two tools: the ministry plan or team charter. Perhaps your outreach no longer matches the needs of your target audience. Maybe you need to add a team member to focus on a different area or bring new perspectives to planning. Or maybe even a new leader to provide a change of direction and renewed zeal. Whatever you do, do not stay stagnant! If you want your ministry to survive, you need to stay fresh and relevant.

What if you do begin to feel like it may be time for the ministry to close up shop? How will you know? Here are some tell-tale signs:

- **Your ministry is running out of people to reach.** Imagine a program that at first was an exciting ministry, bringing many back to Christ. Pastors were enthusiastic and every parish wanted to tap into this ministry's potential. But over the years, the program starts running out of candidates. In fact, there is barely anyone left to choose from! Just about everyone has participated. When a ministry gets to this point, it's time to consider if it has fulfilled its mission, or if the ministry simply needs a change of direction.

- **Your team lacks the stamina and fervor to continue.** Sure, maybe this is due to poor team dynamics, but if you have followed the steps in this book, fatigue shouldn't be the problem. Does your team get more excited about the ministry or the possibility of dedicating their time elsewhere? Have they stopped showing up to planning meetings as often as they did before? Are they starting to focus their efforts on other ministries? The Holy Spirit may be telling us through these signs that the ministry is losing momentum and it's time for something new.

- **You've reached all your goals!** If you were prayerful throughout the planning process, you discerned appropriate goals for your ministry and you have achieved these goals, it could be time to simply say "mission accomplished!" When a company plans an initiative—such as merging two smaller companies together—once the goal is accomplished, there is no need to continue the initiative. Strategic teams brought together for a clear task can be repurposed to focus on the next pressing issue for the organization. Don't think of closing up shop as bad news but as something very exciting—it means you completed the work set out for you!

If you do indeed feel it's time to shutter your ministry, you can either:

1. **Let it decline** – Simply ride it out until it ends. Divert resources, time and energy away from it, serve the last remaining members whom the Lord brings to the cause, then officially end when all momentum comes to a halt; like a boat gently coasting into shore. This can be the least painful for long-invested members, as it allows them to mourn the passing of something good as they prepare to move on.

2. **Close** – Officially end the ministry, making a formal announcement if needed. This is the quickest way to disburse your team into other areas to which they feel called, and the cleanest way to end a ministry rather than just waiting for things to evaporate. One thing to consider is that you may have trouble motivating folks to stay in-

volved if they know the end is in sight.

We've reviewed your options at the "decision point" but now the most important thing of all—how to actually make the right decision! There is only one way to make this choice, and that is through prayer. Spend time alone with our Lord, but bring the following things to Him for discernment:

- **The advice of others** – What do others—particularly your pastor—have to say about your ministry? Do they still think there is more it could do, and if so, what? Or do they also think it is time e to move on?

- **Data** – What's the latest data in your ministry? Is attendance trending up or down? Are more new leaders coming forward or not? In a broader sense, what does current research say about the needs of the Church? Have demographics shifted within your parish boundary, making your ministry less relevant? What are all of the important metrics you can gather to help you make the right decision?

- **Your own feelings** – This is very important and shouldn't be underestimated. How do you feel about the ministry? Are you still excited to get up and work on your initiatives? Or are you starting to feel sluggish? Perhaps the answer is to change leadership; maybe you are the one impeding progress—that is okay and healthy to realize. We'll have done our best work as ministry leaders when we produce other ministry leaders and give them the reins. A ministry should not be dependent upon any of us—it should thrive when we walk away. If you feel God pulling you in this direction, ask Him to show you the new leader to whom you can hand it off to, the one who has the right gifts and talents for the next phase.

If you do make the decision to hand off your ministry to new leadership, this next chapter will be helpful.

CHAPTER 9

UNPACKING THE TRUNK

The maxim for knowing when to unpack the trunk and hand off a ministry is to start with the end in mind. Build your ministry in such a way that it will be ready to hand off one day. Always keep in the back of your mind that the Lord may call you elsewhere and you must leave your nets behind and follow Him. Someone will inherit your ministry after you and you want to do everything in your power to help that person find success at making disciples.

Blueprint Mentality

I (Dan) had the chance to put this into practice while working as the director of campus ministry for several years. The position was brand new and came with the freedom to renovate and re-establish a robust program with a team of talented people so that the ministry could really flourish. I was also in grad school at the time and knew that this job would not be my last. Very likely, it would not last more than a few years.

This meant that the ministry could not be personality-driven, one that was established around the magnetic personality of an inspiring leader (assuming that was even possible). Instead, it needed to provide a nimble yet ample array of ministry experiences that led the students to a deeper relationship with the Lord. The outreach needed to be such that any minister could step in and take over from another person. As much as possible, the experiences needed to be interchangeable with some other format so that if we weren't attracting people or the logistics were not correct, we could pivot quickly and find a better way to connect with the flock.

Without realizing it, I backed into a Flock Experience mentality. I also had the good fortune to create a blueprint for ministry that I could easily hand off to another person and allow him or her to run with it. These two steps are probably inseparable, and we think that these should be included in everything we do.

Maintenance or Mission

As we discussed in the last chapter, we suggest that you examine the existing ministries within your parish on a regular basis to make sure they are on the right track. Are you in maintenance-mode with these ministries, or mission mode? Are you in the win-build-send cycle of discipleship, or have you stalled at one of those stages? A good question to ask: Does this ministry directly or indirectly lead to discipleship, and if so, does it do it well? Does your youth ministry prepare young people to lead others to Christ? Does your fall festival raise enough money relative to the number of volunteer hours, and does this help the overall goal of discipleship?

If, after assessing the core function and value of a ministry, you realize that it is not focused on the mission of making disciples, it might be the right time to hand off a ministry. If you don't, you may look up five years down the road and realize that for the hundreds or maybe thousands of hours you invested, relatively few people were any closer to fulfilling the Great Commission. If that's not why we are in ministry, what are we doing?

When?

Sometimes the question and answer are given to us—we move, there are financial reasons, or we have the birth of a child, etc. We simply can't carry on the ministry as we would wish, so we must hand it off to someone else. In such scenarios, you might not even have the time to get things together. If you started with the end in mind and maintained a Blueprint Mentality, this process will be much easier. Otherwise, you will have just a day or two, at best, to hurriedly explain everything to your replacement or to that friend on staff who is taking over for you part-time. How much nicer would it be to hand them a USB or three-ring binder with a clear path to success? How much easier will it be for someone to take over if everything you do is oriented towards making disciples? A lot!

If you don't already have this plan in place, now is a great time to start so that you have it when you need it. It will probably also turn into a spring-cleaning opportunity and allow you to take a new look at your ministry, deciding what to keep and what not to. We actually recommend something like this once a year where you compare where you are to where you originally wanted to be, making sure that you haven't drifted off target. In the end, this type of reflection becomes an act of virtue (love and justice) for the people we work with and the people who will take over for us. Do it for them, and for the people to whom you minister!

Prayer and Dissatisfaction

Two other reasons why you may hand off a ministry include something you received in prayer and a sense of dissatisfaction with your work. The dissatisfaction could take many forms—boredom, feeling inefficient, sensing a divide between your skills and how you spend your time, or environmental factors like office culture and morale. No matter the cause, we think the appropriate response is prayer—undertaking a disciplined plan of discernment for a set period of time to ask the Lord for clarity.

There are better resources on discernment than we can fit into a chapter section, so we will include the best books and media in the appendices and leave you with a framework. First, we want to say that if you have a very negative relationship in ministry, one that causes anxiety, fear, or some other strong negative emotion, you should talk to a friend or family member that you trust to give you honest feedback. You could also consider talking to a trusted priest or religious therapist, or spiritual director. They can help you discern if your workplace relationships are so bad that the Lord is already giving you a clear answer: get out. Reverently, we offer this advice to both paid ministry personnel and volunteers.

If your dissatisfaction is generalized, not specific, and you just think your ministry could be better, or if the Lord is sharing in prayer to do something different, here is what we recommend. First, pick a period of time for which you can commit to a practice of discernment. This could be as short as one day or could last a couple of weeks. If you tend to drag things out, stick to the shorter end—one day or less. If you are impulsive and would benefit from more time in prayer anyway, choose a longer window.

If you know that you are in a period of dryness or desolation, now is not the time to make a change (assuming there is nothing sinful involved). We have all had days or even consecutive weeks where we think that something isn't going well and we should back out, only to come out of a spiritual slump later. If this is the case, recommit yourself to the practices of living the Gospel that you know God has called you to, seek spiritual counsel from a trusted person, and double down on prayer.

If you aren't in desolation, then continue with the prayer of discernment, asking yourself along the way if your involvement and investment in this ministry brings spiritual peace. If you ask this with honesty and commit yourself to consistent prayer over a set period of time, we are confident that the Lord will reveal to you what you should do. One of the keys to this is that you set a decision point at the end of this period: when your time is up, decide what to do. The beauty of proper discernment is that we trust that the Lord will *always* show us what to do. We need not fear mistakes. If He wants us to do something else, He will let us know!

As you discern, some concerns might arise in your mind and it is good to bring these to the Lord in prayer, as well as to a trusted advisor in the proper domain (spiritual, professional, mental health, etc.). Maybe you are unhappy because you think you aren't qualified. Perhaps you fear someone will find out (imposter syndrome) and you will lose your job. Perhaps you are frustrated because you are trying to grow too fast and you don't see the results you want. Is it possible that you aren't getting the support you need from your supervisor or your team? Maybe you are a control freak and you need to let go of some things so that your team can step up and start hitting home runs!

Finally, perhaps your heart isn't in it anymore. This could be a form of spiritual dryness, but it could also be spiritual lukewarmness, and you probably know the difference. Are you giving God your best (yourself!), or are you just pouring yourself into your ministry like the older son in the parable of the Prodigal (Luke 15:11-32)? Do you expect God's favor because you work hard? If any of these rings true, now is a great time to restart your prayer life and find a spiritual director—he or she will help you rediscover your love for God and the mission that He has just for you.

Handing Off a Ministry

Some basic steps for handing off a ministry well are planning with the end in mind, creating a smooth transition from you to another person, and motivating yourself with a love of your flock, a sense of justice to others, and a love of excellence (Phil 4:8). If you are leaving the parish or organization, this will allow you to stand before God and neighbor, knowing that you acted as Christ would. In the future, you want to be able to maintain healthy relationships with your former co-workers. If you aren't leaving but just transitioning to a new role, maintaining these relationships is even more important, and you will have set an example of Christ for others.

Plan Ahead

The easiest way to hand off a ministry well is to plan ahead! Just planning, period, is the big difference-maker. This means creating systems and documentation that you can hand off to someone else. An image that helps me is looking at my mind like a filing cabinet and my ministry plan like a briefcase. When we set our goals, identify values, and develop a Discipleship Funnel, we take all of the ideas out of the filing cabinet in our head and put those files in a briefcase so that we can easily share them with other people.

The added benefit to this is that we make our ideas clear and explicit enough that we feel comfortable sharing them with other people. We have probably had the experience of trying to articulate our own vision to someone else for the first time: we get frustrated with how fuzzy the concepts and connections are. Those fuzzy spots are actually holes in our ideas and the process of planning and getting them on paper forces us to refine, connect the dots, and fill in areas that are lacking substance and structure.

But there is a second component to planning ahead, and that is remembering that you will not do this ministry forever, and you very likely will not do it for as long as you plan. If you end up staying longer, you will just reap the benefit of a robust systemization and planning process! Imagine trying to recreate an event from ten years earlier without documentation to go by! Or you may be forced to leave sooner than you wish: health, loss of job, transfer, etc. So, whether you are creating reminders for yourself or for your replacement, following the frameworks in this book, documenting your systems, and planning meetings, changes, expenses, etc., will help your ministry succeed and help others create true disciples. That is moving the needle!

This is also an antidote to pride, as you are forced to make the ministry about discipleship rather than yourself. By now, you have probably seen a ministry that is personality-based. There is a good chance that when that magnetic personality left, the ministry collapsed. We should keep in mind the words of St. Paul, "What is Apollos, after all, and what is Paul ... I planted, Apollos watered, but God caused the growth" (1 Cor 3:5-6). We are called to witness to Christ, not to ourselves, and if we can't easily hand off our ministry to another, are we being faithful to the Gospel?

Smooth Transition

When someone takes over for you, you want that person to succeed. Helping the new person succeed is an act of Christian charity, and his or her success will be great for your flock. The more capable he or she seems as a leader, the more people will encounter the Lord. You can help him or her win by systematizing and documenting your process, choosing a clear date to hand everything over, and then getting out of the way. You can still be there for support, but make sure it is clear that he or she is in charge. Remember, you may have to continue working with this person for a long time, and may even end up working for him or her in the future!

The date for the handoff doesn't have to be months into the future, but it also doesn't need to be today at 2:00 p.m. The nature of the job will dictate how long you need to train and transition the new person in and yourself out. Two weeks seems to us like the maximum length, assuming you have the opportunity to train your replacement. This may include formal training on how to lead the ministry, as well as shadowing and guided practice. You simply can't explain each scenario and aspect of your work and expect the person to remember everything. It would be far better preparation to give your replacement a big picture and introduction to your plan, and then work side-by-side so he or she gets a taste of the issues that may arise.

Once these steps are completed, step back and step out of the way. Well done, good and faithful servant; your successor will be grateful for the effort you made to help him or her succeed. If you had the secret hope of being invited back as a guest later on, you just did everything in your power to increase the likelihood of receiving that invite. This very thing happened to me (Dan). I was invited to deliver a graduation commencement address at the high school where I had previously worked. Even though I had been eager to take a new job with greater responsibility, I made a commitment to excellence in my final weeks because it was the virtuous thing to do. The graduation keynote was affirmation that I left the right way!

Love of Your flock

For our money, the clearest reason for wanting to hand ministry off well is love of your flock. Scripture is clear that it is the Lord, not the minister, who is the primary agent of conversion, spiritual growth, and maturity. We play a small part, and if we really want to follow Christ, our primary motivation will be the good of those to whom we minister. Someone else will come after us, witnessing to the love of God and pouring His grace into others to produce fruit in their lives. It is a gift to be a part of another's story, and any temptation towards selfishness or pride comes only from one source, and that is most certainly not the Lord.

If you find yourself experiencing selfishness, pride, or protectiveness, we reverently suggest that you recommit yourself to a deep love of your flock, praying even more fervently for their spiritual growth. Most importantly, pray for the new minister who is taking over for you. Pray, that he or she might be a humble and willing servant of the Lord who labors tirelessly for the kingdom of God. Remember, our Lord said to those who follow Him, "Amen, I say to you, there is no one who has given up house or wife or brothers or parents or children for the sake of the kingdom of God who will not receive an overabundant return in this present age and eternal life in the age to come (Luke 18:29-30).

Planning with the End in Mind

If our ministry is not about making disciples, what is it about? We need to make sure that our ministry follows Christ's model, and that is one of discipleship: attracting, inviting, informing, and forming people who know and love God and who want to make Him known and loved by others.

When we hand off a ministry, we might find an ideal time to reformulate it so that it follows Christ's model. It could be painful to admit on your way out that you weren't headed in the right direction, but what better gift to leave for your successor and for your flock than to make the ministry about the one thing that we need: Jesus. If your ministry is not one that forms disciples, any time is the right time to get back on track.

It might be the case that your ministry was headed in the right direction but there were still areas in need of work. We know from our own experience that there were elements in our previous ministries that needed to be transformed. Other forces were so strong that we were not able to change everything on our own and in our time. It wasn't until we handed the reins to someone else and shared our shortcoming that the ministry was able to grow as God intended. Some plant, others water, others till the soil, but it is God who gives the growth (1 Cor 3:6). No matter where you are in your ministry, trust that the Lord will provide for whoever takes over. Hold nothing back from Him, or from whoever steps into your shoes.

Ministry Handoff Do's and Don'ts

Do:

1. Start with the end in mind.
2. Document your plans, changes, and initiatives as you go.
3. Prayerfully discern when the Lord wants you to step back.
4. Keep discipleship as the focus of everything you do.

Don't:

1. Leave your replacement high and dry by not providing a map to your ministry.
2. Make the handoff any longer than it has to be.
3. Make a big decision on a bad day. Wait until you are in spiritual equilibrium to discern and decide.

CHAPTER 10

WHAT'S NEXT?

Christ invites each one of us to follow Him, to say yes to making Him present in the world. The Blessed Mother, a simple young girl to whom Christ made the same offer, gave such a complete yes that she ushered in the Salvation of every human being that has ever existed and ever will exist. Now, while we don't want to overwhelm you with the magnitude of this choice, we say this to remind you of the splendor and dignity of God's invitation. This is an invitation to play a major role in His plan to bring about the Salvation of the world. Even a partial and incomplete yes could result in thousands upon thousands of people turning to the Lord, receiving His gift of Salvation, and lining up to shake your hand in heaven.

Whatever you do next, we invite you to consider organizing your life and your pastoral activity (that is, your ministry) around Christ. We invite you to do this using the same principles and frameworks that we have shared with you for organizing and planning your ministry. We put these frameworks together to help you keep the big picture of discipleship at the center of your ministry, to move the needle by reversing the trend of disaffiliation for the Church. But before we succeed in that arena, we need Christ to be the center of our own lives even more than we need Him to be the center of our ministry. As much as we want to transform our world, the first thing we must transform is our own hearts. Discipleship starts with us; we cannot pass on what we do not have.

First, consider what the future flock of the Church needs. How are they to be engaged, evangelized, and brought into relationship with Christ? Consider the Discipleship Funnel, what constitutes outreach, and what relationship building looks like in your life. Are you a full-time paid minister or you are sanctifying the world in a secular setting? How can you begin making true disciples?

Next, you can ask yourself the 5 Ws: why are you Catholic? Who you are trying to serve, both in terms of who you are doing this for, God, and who you are trying to bring to Him? What would interest these people and how do your unique talents, interests, and abilities help you attract others to the Gospel? Where can you find these people? Just as importantly, when can you make time in your busy life to share the Gospel with them?

While there are dozens of examples of Jesus explaining how to live a good life, we think His last words are normative. These constitute His final mission for His followers: "Go, therefore, and make disciples of all nations, baptizing them in the name of the Father, and of the Son, and of the Holy Spirit, teaching them to observe all that I have commanded you. And behold, I am with you always, until the end of the age" (Matt. 28:19-20). We are confident that you can use these frameworks to help you organize your life so that you can go into the world and do just as Jesus said.

But for any of this to work, Christ must be not only the center of our ministry, but the center of our lives. What follows is a set of questions about how you could discern the next step in dedicating your life to God, and like Mary, give Him a yes that has the potential to change the course of human history.

What Does the Church Need?

Scripture and the Popes are clear: the Church exists to evangelize. Jesus modeled this to His disciples while He was still on earth. He sent them out two by two to practice, and He modeled it even after the Resurrection. While on the road to Emmaus, He showed us what it means to walk with people, to accompany them to a mature faith in the midst of their doubt, even their denial of Christ. All recent Popes have been univocal in reminding and encouraging the entire Church to regain a missionary focus. Everything else she does, including her mission of mercy, is oriented towards the mission of evangelization. If we took these words seriously, ". . . we would realize that missionary outreach is *[the model] for all the Church's activity*" (Evang. Gaud., 15).

The Church's very reason for being is to bring people into relationship with Christ and to show them what it means to live as Christ lived. The apostles understood this, as one can clearly see in the book of Acts. The entire book is a verbal image, a picture in words of the ripple effect across all space and time from the momentous event of the Resurrection. The apostles spread throughout the world, announcing the Good News of forgiveness of sins brought about by the suffering, death, and resurrection of Jesus. They took it so seriously that eleven of the twelve went to their deaths to make Jesus known, as did Saint Paul and countless other faithful witnesses.

The Church is telling us to get out there and do something! A litmus test that I like to use for myself is, "When is the last time I invited somebody to become Catholic?" Or, "When is the last time that I was successful in helping somebody become Catholic?" If the answer to the first question is, "more than a month" and to the second question, "more than a year," I'm probably not making discipleship a priority in my life.

There's a funny saying that circulates in graduate theology classes. "What is the role of the laity?" someone asks. The response: "The Church would look silly without them." The point of this joke is to remind people that any theology of the Church needs a view of the lay faithful that goes beyond, "The laity are there to pay, pray, and obey." Here's how deep this thinking runs. While teaching a high school theology class, I (Dan) once asked students to design a Catholic role-playing board game. One student created characters based on the different vocations in the life of the Church. All of the characters had superpowers . . . except the laity. They simply supported the efforts of the Church through financial contributions.

We need a similar joke to remind us that our vision of the Church needs a clear injunction, an outward surge that obliges us to make disciples. All of us. No one can avoid this responsibility. No one has the luxury of assuming that the whole world has sufficiently heard of the love of the Father, proclaimed in the story of the Son, and made real by the power of the Holy Spirit. We don't have to be good at it, but we still need to do it.

At times, the Church feels like a barracks full of soldiers who are constantly training for battle and yet never have the opportunity to fight. How long can we carry on without eventually turning upon one another to vent our aggression? This is already visible in the factions (or fractions!) that exist within the body of Christ. Saint Paul reminded us that we belong to Christ alone, not to this or that famous teacher or apostle (1 Cor 1:12). What would Jesus say about us today?

Another image that comes to mind is that of some large machine. It has an engine at the center with many inter-connecting and moving parts that, when working together, achieve some wonderful end. But what if the purpose of the machine is not met and it has no output? All of that energy must go somewhere, and it will eventually tear the machine apart. Rather than expanding its energy moving something towards the target, it simply reverberates with its own force and shakes itself to pieces. Here are two similar examples: a bow that is pulled under tension and then released with no arrow is likely to snap, and a car with its wheels lifted off the floor and the pedal blocked all the way down will eventually explode. Let us pray that this might not happen to us!

How beautiful would it be if we as a Church were so busy proclaiming the word of God that we didn't have time to debate?

What Does the World Need?

Ok, so the clarion call of Christ and His Church is to evangelize. But this is a big picture answer to the question of what the Church needs and not one that gives us actionable steps. How do we make it simpler?

Evangelization means finding people who haven't heard the message of Jesus and sharing it with them. It also means finding people who have already heard the Gospel, but for whom it has grown old and lost its saltiness. For these people, we must make the Gospel sound new again. But we can hardly even know where to begin with such a massive undertaking. So here are some ideas about how you can refine your efforts based on what we see as most needed in the world.

On a practical level, the Church needs people to go where the Gospel has not yet been proclaimed. We are talking about the Internet, today's version of the Athenian marketplace where Saint Paul preached the Gospel (Acts 17: 16-34). In some ways, this is the part of the world that is least interested in the message of Jesus but simultaneously most willing to engage in conversation. Remember, our mission is to the lost sheep (Matt 15:24), to those people who have wandered far and about whom Jesus says, "There is more rejoicing in heaven over one sinner who repents than over the ninety-nine who had no need of repentance" (Luke 15:3-7).

Following the model of the Good Shepherd, let us venture into the wilderness. Sure, there are still plenty of physical areas in the world where the Gospel hasn't really been preached, but the distance between you and every other human being has been so dramatically decreased by the Internet that you can now evangelize practically everyone from your home. This comes with virtually no risk to your own life, something that would have amazed the early Christians.

Consider how many resources in terms of hours and dollars you put towards reaching out to non-Catholics on the Internet, especially those who live within a twenty-minute drive of your parish. There may be an online community already established for people who live near you. It might exist for some unique purpose like garage sales or gardeners, but why not become interested in that topic if doing so brings more people to the Lord? After all, Saint Paul encourages us to become all things to all people in order that we might win some for Christ (1 Cor 9:19-23).

What follows is a shortlist of recommended areas that we think are likely to bear fruit if we invest sufficient resources in them.

Beauty

The slowest form of evangelization is to gradually expose people to the goodness of God revealed in beauty. If you are an artist, we need you. We need you to harness the gifts that God is giving you to make the invisible visible. Please, reveal to the world the hidden glory of God that waits like a seed within every created thing, bird, beast, and flower, anxious to burst forth onto the scene and shout to the world of the goodness of God.

Not all of us can do this. If you can, you are extraordinarily lucky, gifted, and needed. We need you. We need you to beautify our churches, both inside and out, in-person and online. When someone first encounters us, whether driving by or browsing social media, they need to be moved by our care and concern for detail, order, harmony, and beauty. Jesus said, "Let he who has ears hear"(Matt 11:15). We would be so bold as to say, "Let he who has eyes see." If you have the eyes to see the latent beauty in the world around us, please, please, please, do us all the favor of pointing it out, highlighting it, and showing us the transcendent splendor of God.

Parish Discipleship Teams

I know it should be clear that we think everybody should be actively making disciples. But what is the elephant in the room? Everyone knows we need to do this, but few actually know how. Imagine if someone walked into your high school algebra class with a calculus textbook and asked you to start solving equations. That might sound like fun to some of you (or not), but many of us wouldn't even know how to begin. So how do we go from where we are to where we want to be? What every parish needs is a team of people who are naturally gifted teachers and leaders who can be trained as—and then train more—missionary disciples.

But how do you train these people if you don't have disciple-makers already? What if you have to lead them and you don't even know how? You just have to go through the process yourself. What follows is an adaptation of the process we went through to become disciples of Christ. If you follow it, we are confident that it will lead you deeper and lead to a deep encounter with Him. If you can find someone to guide you through this process, all the better.

First, talk to the pastor about this plan and get his approval. Ask him for the names of seven or eight people who are FCAT: faithful, contagious, available, and teachable. These attributes predispose people to the process of discipleship.

Why these? If you are discipling people who are already Catholic or Christian (bringing them into the Church), they need some level of *faithfulness* to Christ and His teaching. If they aren't yet Christian, look for at least some level of openness to faith. *Availability* refers to life circumstances: does he or she have four kids under five? If so, now might not be the right time. There is a season for everything, and since you can't disciple everyone, you look for those who can give their time and heart to God *now*. He will provide for the others later. *Teachable* is another way of saying open, docile, malleable, and humble—if they have all the answers, if they are not sick, if they are already righteous, then they don't know they need the Messiah (Mark 2:17). This is out of order, by why *contagious*? While everyone needs to hear the Gospel, contagious people will increase our impact. These are the people that everyone wants to be around because they are fun, likeable, good listeners, friend-makers, community builders, etc.

Once the pastor gives you the names, give them a call or take them out to coffee. Ask if they would be interested in joining a small discipleship group that is intentional about learning how to follow more closely in the footsteps of Jesus and intentionally share the faith with other people.

Once people have said yes, commit to meeting regularly, either together or one-on-one. During this time, you apprentice these people into an intentional Christian life: you study the word of God, you learn to pray together, you fellowship and have a great time together, and you find ways of serving those in need. This description of life comes directly from Acts of the Apostles, 2:42-47. It is a simple job description of what it looks like to be Catholic and to be in communion with one another. This happened spontaneously (under the guidance of the Spirit) when people fell in love with the Lord. They were inspired by His love to worship together, to study His Word, and learn as much about Him as they could. Together, they took care of those in need and became true friends.

If you spend some time thinking about this framework of word, worship, fellowship, and service, you will find creative and flexible ways to fit this into your own life. For others, the way you live will become a novel and appealing window into the life of Christ and His Church. In time, you will arouse a newfound desire in others to consider following Christ.

Over the course of six to eighteen months, the goal is to become so immersed in the life of Christ such that you and your group fall in love with Him and His Gospel. The balance of study and prayer, fellowship, and service, as you engage mind and body will gradually reveal that the faith is not *simply* an intellectual pursuit—it is incarnational, for it involves the whole human person. Jesus became man so that man might become God (St. Athanasius, On the Incarnation, 54:3). This means that Jesus came to redeem the entire human experience, not just give us a mental state of bliss to distract us from our current suffering. Christianity is the transformation of the entire human experience. In following Christ, we step into the eternal and infinite experience of the Holy Trinity, into its eternal exchange of love, perfection, and goodness. This is what makes Christianity so different. We don't need to steal fire from the gods—God has come down to us to give us His very lifeblood and draw us unto Himself.

As you and your group experience the foretaste of the redemption of your humanity, you will start to take on a different character and to become attractive to those around you. This will lead to the questions and curiosity of others, and these very people are the next participants in the discipleship process. Within six to eighteen months, your group will be ready to branch off and start their own ministry. The appropriate timeline will look different for everyone, but you will probably have a good idea when people are ready. When they are, do what Jesus did and send them out on their own, trusting that the Lord will be the one at work in them.

For more resources to guide you and your disciples in training, check out the list of resources at the end of the

book. We didn't want you to have to read another book before you got started, but the resources we list will help tre-
mendously along the way.

Families

After proclaiming the Gospel, the thing the world needs
most is helping families ensure the faithfulness of the next
generation of Catholics. This conclusion is based upon
long term research into the lives of religious and former re-
ligiously affiliated young Americans. The most important
factor in predicting whether young people will continue
to practice the faith of their upbringing is their parents'
commitment, devotion, and faithfulness. Also vital is the
parents' ability to establish a family culture that intentionally presents the Catholic faith as a valuable, meaning-
giving, guiding framework for moving through life.

Parents who are successful at transmitting their faith
tend to do four things, all of which are important. First,
they are reflective about their own experience of faith
and religious belief, and they have a narrative-like view of
what God has done and what *He will do*. They hope that
God will continue to be present in their own lives and
that He will bring their whole family into *His* narrative of
salvation. In short, they know and reflect upon the truth
that God made their lives infinitely better and worth living, and they want their spouse and children to experience
the same thing. To make this personal, think of the most
fulfilling experience in prayer or the most breath-taking
encounter with beauty you've ever had. Isn't it the most
obvious thing in the world that you want your loved ones
to have the same experiences? We need to be as clear and
convicted about the value that our faith will bring to our
family members.

Next, successful parents have both a macro- and micro-level view of *how* and *what* they will share with their children. The *how* refers to the overarching structure, the rule of life and components of family culture. This merely starts with regular attendance of Sunday Mass, and from there should flourish naturally according to the creativity and unique interests of the family. How do you incorporate a rich experience of prayer as individuals and as a family? How do you study more about God and make Him a part of regular family discussions? How do you live the teachings of the Gospel, especially serving those in need? Parents must work to establish an alternate culture to the dominant one, a culture within the home that points to Christ as the only one worthy of a total sacrifice of our life. Contrast His enduring perfection and appeal with the various idols secular culture offers and He will always win!

Finally, just as in the discipleship process, parents will need to allow their children to venture forth and encounter God on their own. This means providing opportunities for an encounter with the Lord on retreats, in youth groups, and summer adventure camps. These are what we like to call mountain-top experiences. These help young people move from seeing the Catholic faith as a beautiful philosophy for life to having an intimate, loving relationship with Christ. A positive perception of the Church is fundamental, but it is just a steppingstone to a life-long, committed relationship with Christ.

For ministry leaders, the four areas of word, worship, fellowship, and service provide a framework for helping to form families. These are the building blocks of the Christian life and they reveal a path that is rich with possibilities for ministry. Your role will be to show forth the beauty of our Catholic faith and its vision of family life, revealing its power to transform and elevate life. This will help parents see the rich tapestry of Catholic culture that they can sew into the fabric of their home life.

The problem won't be what to do, it will be choosing from among the near-infinite set of resources that our faith has to offer. Which saints can families read about? They can choose from knights in armor to desert monks and mystics, from former killers to former slaves, from young virgins to faithful spouses, from the whole range of human experiences.

What about prayer? Our tradition is rich beyond belief. This is something of a secret to a world that is increasingly enamored with spirituality even as it attempts to abandon religion. Western meditation was started by the first Catholic hermits and mystics who encountered the infinite goodness of God in their solitude and simplicity. This rich spiritual life was so attractive that it spawned the entire monastic tradition of Christianity. From this came the rich interior life of Carmelite spirituality, the psychological genius of Ignatian prayer and discernment, the perfect simplicity of the Rosary, the liturgy of the hours, and the list goes on. Let's bring out these treasures of the faith and put them on display to a world that is desperately seeking to encounter God!

"The poor will always be with you" (Mark 14:7), as Jesus reminds us, and so there will never be a shortage of ways for families to meet Jesus in His "distressing disguises" (St. Theresa of Calcutta) in the poorest of the poor. As for fellowship, this will rise up spontaneously, but good places to start are the renewal of liturgical celebrations, and not just the big ones. Holding parties or neighborhood barbeques on the occasion of a name-sake day or baptism are ways of living what we believe, transforming our thoughts into reality.

If you are a parent reading this, whether or not you work for the Church, we hope that we have provided another framework to create your very own Catholic family culture, one that successfully transmits the faith. We hope that you always remember that you are the most important person in your child's life, *especially* in handing on our beloved faith. As with ministry, start with the end in mind and then map out your course, being deliberate and reflective along the way. You can do this!

Social Justice

While social justice, social justice warrior, and other related terms have become common today, the Christian witness of concern for the poor and marginalized has been powerful throughout our entire history. Jesus's own love and attention to the downtrodden attracted the attention of many, including His enemies, but it also won Him followers (see the story of Bartimaeus in Mark 10:46-52). Or look to the radical witness of St. Francis and the reformative impact his regard for the poor had on the Church, or to Mother Theresa who was respected worldwide. When we love as Jesus loves, we attract attention because we look like Him, and He was the single most remarkable and attractive human to ever walk the earth.

For reasons we don't claim to understand, there seems to be an awakening among many young people, including those who have left the Church, that we are in fact our brother's keeper. They see this not just individually but in a systematic, far-reaching manner. Eco-conscious, fair-trade, and otherwise "ethically" inspired products are now commonplace in supermarkets throughout the country because consumers hear in their conscience the call to look after both neighbor and creation. This door is wide open for evangelization.

If you are more passionate about other issues, such as the pro-life movement, the economy, etc., I invite you to consider this situation. Let's say you board a plane from Orlando to Los Angeles, a pretty long flight, and right next to you is a young person who looks to be fresh out of college. His laptop is covered with stickers, including several that identify him as a member of the "other" party. You want to share your faith, but you are tempted to bring up *your* favorite topics. These topics align with your political leanings, which you assume your new neighbor will be opposed to.

Before you get started, ask yourself this question. By the end of the flight, what do you really want to happen? Do you want that person to be a little more open to Jesus, or do you want him to join your political party? Our goal should always be the former, and this means we don't have to argue every point. Instead, we build trust.

In social justice, we may find a lot of common ground with non-Catholics. Letting them know that we see eye-to-eye on some things can be an easy way to develop trust. If we come in ready for battle on this or that topic, our airplane buddy is going to go into fight or flight mode. If, on the other hand, we build a bridge by discussing our shared concern for the poor, the marginalized, etc., it is a natural and easy step to discuss how Jesus is the one who inspires us.

Social justice is an open door. If they hear our rationale (which is beautiful and crystalline) and see our witness in service, the stereotypes that he or she has of a Catholic will begin to evaporate. From the mist of misconception will start to emerge the person of Christ.

What Do You Have to Offer?

We aren't good at or passionate about all of the areas listed above, and you probably aren't either. Most of the time, we don't have time to work on all of them or even several of them. That is okay, and this is where good discernment comes in. If you need a reminder on how to do this, go back and visit chapter nine, or check out some of the recommended resources. We are confident that the Lord will reveal to you, if He hasn't already, how you can serve Him. We are also confident that this dedication will include things that you are passionate about, or that you will become passionate about when you engage in them.

Listed above are the most pressing needs of the Church and the world as we see it. The arch principle in all of this is evangelization. Our Lord and the Church are clear on this: evangelization is the first mission and goal of the Church and the reason for her existence. What remains is to take time to examine your own relationship with the Lord. Ask Him to reveal to you the nexus between your unique talents and the needs of the world.

We pray that you order your life in such a way that Christ is at the center. We pray that your missionary discipleships begin with His Gospel and bring people back to it, back to Him. The image that comes to mind is a wagon wheel: the all-important hub keeping everything in tension and delivering strength and support to the outer circumference, the spokes connecting our entire lived reality to the heart of our existence, Jesus Christ. A more refined image is that of the rose stained-glass window. Christ is at the center with so many resplendent aspects of the faith shining forth from Him. May the rose window pale in comparison to the beauty of your own life with Christ.

Be assured of our prayers for you and everyone to whom you gift this book.

Now that you finished reading *Go! Make Disciples*, it's time to start doing it. For Him.

APPENDIX A

Resources for collecting data

Surveys are a powerful tool for understanding your target audience. The following is a sample of the types of information you can gather.

Demographics

Demographic information helps you understand your target audience better. Knowing who attends your outreach can help you lock on to the target flock. Here are some examples of demographic information you can gather.

- Gender
- Primary language
- Age range
- Religion
- City or state of residence
- Commute time
- Marital status
- Family information

Pre and Post or Change Surveys

These types of surveys let you see how effective your efforts are. With a pre and post survey, you gather information before and after your outreach. A change survey can be done after your outreach, but you will still ask questions about their beliefs or habits before and after an outreach. Here are some examples that could have been used on a retreat to help people return to confession, pray more, or develop a closer relationship with God.

- How frequently did you attend confession before this outreach?
- Please rate the likeliness that you will go to confession more often.
- How likely were you to pray daily before attending?
- Please rate your new desire to pray daily.
- How close did you feel to God before the retreat?
- How close do you feel to God now?

General Survey Questions

These questions can be used in many settings and it is much easier to create a survey from a bank of questions than it is to write them from scratch. Feel free to add these to your database.

Outreach Related

- What was your (least) favorite part of this outreach? (Free response)
- How likely are you to return to an outreach like this? (Very likely-very unlikely scale)
- How likely are you to recommend this outreach to a friend? (Very likely-very unlikely scale)
- Did this outreach improve your relationship with God? How so? (1-10 scale with free response)
- The cost of participation was appropriate. (Strongly agree-strongly disagree scale)
- I was satisfied with the food. (Strongly agree-strongly disagree scale)
- The length of the entire outreach was appropriate. (Strongly agree-strongly disagree scale)

- The length of each presentation was appropriate (Strongly agree-strongly disagree scale)

Speaker Related

- The speaker was prepared. (Strongly agree-strongly disagree scale)
- The speaker was knowledgeable. (Strongly agree-strongly disagree scale)
- The speaker stayed on schedule and used time well. (Strongly agree-strongly disagree scale)
- I would come back to hear this speaker again. (Strongly agree-strongly disagree scale)

APPENDIX B

Core Values Bank

Organizations tend to write core values in two different ways: using singular adjectives, or as short statements that look more like "core beliefs." Whichever format you choose, having these defined for your ministry will help set direction and define culture. Here are some examples:

As singular adjectives:

1. Trust – be open and honest with all members without fear of repercussion

2. Unity – though we may dialogue on issues we leave meetings unified in our stance

3. Orthodoxy – we are faithful to the magisterium of the church

4. Marian – we place all initiatives under the mantle of Mary and promote devotion to her

5. Christ-centered – Christ is the center of all we do and all initiatives lead back to Him

6. Prayerful – we pray as a team and individually so that everything is done in a spirit of prayer

7. Dialogue – we dialogue and listen to each other and everyone we meet

8. High-quality – we strive for excellence in all we do

9. Diversity – we create outreach for all people within our target market so none feel left out

10. Research-based – our work is based on research, not just our opinions

As short statements (with sample ministry):

1. All Catholics should evangelize (for an outreach motivating Catholics to share their faith)

2. Christ is present in our daily lives (for an outreach promoting prayerful families)

3. We go after the lost sheep (for serving those with addictions)

4. God gives us the tools we need (for a ministry relying on donations or volunteers)

5. Social justice demands legal change (for a pro-life advocacy group)

6. The Bible is for everyone (for a street evangelization group)

7. All have something to add (for a senior citizen outreach group)

8. Conversations are essential (for an RCIA inquiry group)

9. Never give up (for a homeless ministry outreach)

10. Christ is present in the hungry (for a food pantry)

Additional Core Values

Prudence

Justice

Temperance

Fortitude

Charity

Diligence

Patience

Mercy

Hope

Faith

Wonder

Beauty in All Things

Perseverance

Humor

Biblical

Tradition

Creativity

Transparency

Consistency

Passion

Holiness

Willing to Fail

People Focused

Communication

Develop Leadership

Trust

Accountable

Adaptable

Friendship

Fraternity

Joyful

Missionary

Accompaniment

Growth Mindset

Other-Focused

Humility

Pious

Efficient

Focused

Urgency

Kindness

Wisdom

Meekness

Honesty

Innovative

Vulnerable

Family

Communal

Me-Second

APPENDIX C

Our Top Books for Spiritual and Pastoral Growth

Justin's List

1. *The Bible, especially the Gospel of Mark.* If you have never read a Gospel all the way through, start with Mark, since it is action-packed and the shortest one.
2. *The Discernment of Spirits* by Fr. Timothy M. Gallagher, O.M.V.. Easy-to-understand guide for how to make decisions. Mastering this guide will change your life.
3. *33 Days to Morning Glory* by Fr. Michael E. Gaitley, MIC. A great first step in deepening one's relationship with the Virgin Mary
4. *Consecration to St. Joseph* by Fr. Donald Calloway, MIC. An action-packed ride in discovering the treasure that is our spiritual father St. Joseph!
5. *Wild at Heart by John Eldredge. Spiritual classic on what it means to be a man.*
6. *The Imitation of Christ.* Classic and timeless instruction for growth in the spiritual walk.
7. *Interior Freedom* by Jacques Philippe. Learning to let go and let God work on us through our daily interactions, challenges, and struggles.
8. *Mere Christianity by C.S. Lewis. Clear and concise apologetics on the basics of Christianity.*